(Re)Value

(Re)Value

Raise Your Prices and Build Your Legacy

Adam Wallace (American) with Adam Wallace (Australian)

BEP

BUSINESS EXPERT PRESS

Leader in applied, concise business books

(Re)Value: Raise Your Prices and Build Your Legacy

First published in 2024 by
Business Expert Press, LLC
222 East 46th Street, New York, NY 10017
www.businessexpertpress.com

ISBN-13: 978-1-63742-606-7 (paperback)
ISBN-13: 978-1-63742-607-4 (e-book)

Business Expert Press Human Resource Management and Organizational Behavior Collection

First edition: 2024

10 9 8 7 6 5 4 3 2 1

Thank you to:

My father, the son of a dairy farmer, who always embodied the value of thinking for yourself and still asks really good questions to this day.

My wife, the woman I choose every day and the person who chooses to bring unwavering support in all of our endeavors.

My mother, who has always brought a soft touch to the hard drive for growing beautiful things.

Doug and Lucinda, for the opportunities provided, I am grateful for the support and endorsement.

John, Nicholas, Caleb, and Eric, for providing feedback and insight into shaping the all-important early drafts of this book.

And Adam, for a partner in values and delight to collaborate with, a true mensch.

Description

Pricing power is a simple concept, yet so many successful people overlook it, leaving money on the table. It's not about charging more; **it's about discovering the only type of value your customers will pay more for.**

Not all value is equal. Want to 2X your earnings? If you operate with a 15-percent profit margin, you could grow your business by 100 percent, managing twice the resources and doubling your complexity. Or you could simply increase your pricing power by 15 percent. While few know how, the companies, leaders, and productive individuals embracing the lessons of re-valuing do it every day.

Join the re-value revolution and ignite your team to:

- Discover what your customers are willing to pay more for.
- Identify where your business is leaking value and intervene.
- Cut through competing priorities by asking the right questions.
- Ensure your strategies will stand the test of time.

Re-value shares a wealth of game-changing insights within an easy-to-apply framework, distilling a 20+ year pursuit into an entertaining read that you can easily digest on your next domestic plane ride.

Keywords

how to raise prices; re-value business book; how can you increase prices without losing customers; charging for your expertise; how much should I raise my prices; how do you make a price change; how to improve profit margins in business; what is the best way to increase profit margin; how do companies get pricing power; how do you build pricing power; how do you change perception of value; what affects perceived value; what are ways to enhance perception of value; how do I set prices for my business; why do great businesses fail; what is re-valuing in business; how do you re-value a company; what is meant by re-valuing how a company runs; what does value leakage mean; is it a good idea to raise prices; should you raise your prices every year

Contents

Prologue..xi

Acknowledgments..xiii

Chapter 1   Opening...1

                   Why Now and Why Re-Value? 1

                   Opportunity and Overview 5

Chapter 2   Worthwhile Obstacles.......................................9

                   The Parable of Cash the Cow–Part I...............10

                   Don't Slip on the Monetization Curve............16

                   Avoid Pricing Riptides 21

Chapter 3   Atomic Behaviors 29

                   What Grips Your Attention? 32

                   The Most Overlooked Pricing Variable...........40

                   How to Maximize What They'll Pay 46

Chapter 4   Re-Value Reliably 53

                   Optimize to Your Size, Age, and Knowledge...54

                   Find Your Transparent Thread 61

                   The Simple Process of Re-Valuing 67

Chapter 5   True Questions 73

                   The Parable of Cash the Cow–Part II 73

                   The Most Valuable Type of Question to Ask ...76

                   True Cases and Cautionary Tales 81

Epilogue: The Parable of Cash the Cow–Part III....................91

References..97

About the Authors..99

Index 101

Prologue

What's It Worth?

The amount we value something is never inherent to the thing itself. Take your favorite pair of sunglasses as an example. How much are they worth to you? Maybe they're your favorite because they're the only ones you've ever found that truly balance out your facial features. They could be a vintage pair given to you by someone close, and they bring back fond memories every time you put them on. Or maybe they're just a cheap pair, but they're the only ones that don't hurt your nose after a day of wearing them. It's surprising how small things can make such a big difference in what we value.

There's also an inherent difference between how much we value something and our willingness to exchange cash for that value at any given time. If we wanted to calculate the objective value of your sunglasses, we might take a first-principles approach and start by summing the market cost of the raw material they contain and the value added through manufacturing. Depending on the brand, we might include additional value for the decades of experience and intellectual property (IP) that make this particular pair more comfortable or durable than other options on the market. Of course, we also need to consider the value of the retail experience and, possibly, the cachet of the label or designer.

But, if you were to lose your favorite pair of sunglasses today, it's doubtful you would think about any of those measures in determining what it's worth to replace them. You might even pay a premium price for a no-name brand at a gift store before heading out for a sunny day of boating. Or, if we were to tell you we knew a local kid who was willing to retrace your steps for a $75 reward if he found them, you might very well take that offer—even if you could find a nearly identical used pair on eBay for $50. This is an example of the difference between traditional *explicit* valuation and what we, as individuals, are *implicitly* willing to spend our money on.*

---

*This is also an example of the Endowment Effect.

Economists have long been fascinated by this paradox and have tried to address it with the concept of *utility*. One of the first people to do so was John Stuart Mill, who described utility as a measure of pleasure or happiness one gains from a good or service. Over the years, the concept has been narrowed and redefined to allow for the measurement and modeling of a person's preference out of a defined set of explicit choices. But it still leaves a lot of whitespace between effective modeling of selected variables and the implicit motivations that govern the way your customers live their everyday lives and spend their money.

If you want to improve your pricing, it will mean embracing the unpredictable variables in human nature, not trying to "fix" them in either sense of the word—not trying to improve the way they work or stop them from changing. Digital technology and globalization-induced efficiencies have created an explosion of customer niches in today's business landscape—making our traditional valuation models even less effective for calculating what a subset of people are willing to actually pay for an item on the ever-expanding margins. A simple, reliable way to predict and validate implicit valuing of your offering at the individual level might now offer outsized rewards as you work to optimize your offering to the marketplace.

To revisit the sunglasses example, say someone finds your lost pair cleaning out a lost and found box. Understandably placing so little value on them, that person is debating between donating them to Goodwill or just tossing them in the trash. However, say at that moment, I walk by and recognize the pair as your long-lost favorite. I inform this person that not only are these your sunglasses, but they were given to you by Elton John. Instantly, the value they place on them changes. I go on to share that Elton wore them the night he first sang "Tiny Dancer" at a little British nightclub, and that crack in the right lens? That happened when he walked out of the club, and the local police arrested him for drug possession and roughed him up a bit. Imagine the value of that pair of sunglasses now. No one would ever contemplate throwing them away.

The amount we value something is never inherent to the thing itself.

This monograph is focused on the often under-attended variables that enable you to capture and keep more earnings from the value you already create every day.

Acknowledgments

To my son Ronan,

The horizon in my life's journey has just shifted from counting up to calculating down. Yours has just begun, toddling into my office babbling your first words as I type these.

It will be a great joy for me to see you grow into your own. But just in case I fall short and am no longer alive when you do, I end this book with what I wish to be able to say to you then.

CHAPTER 1

Opening

Why Now and Why Re-Value?

*A **Riddle**: What product has come to dominate the business landscape over the past two decades? It's been manufactured by tens of thousands of companies, each with its own variant. However, this product is so ubiquitous that it may have oversaturated the market without notice, and its outsized impact on expected business strategy has attracted surprisingly little attention.*

Answer: The company itself. In reflection, it may not be so strange to think about a company as a product. After all, a product is simply something that's manufactured or refined to be sold. How many companies are created or bought every day with the sole purpose of being resold? If this is the overarching goal, it shouldn't surprise us that this factor can shape how the company's offerings get developed and priced.

Of course, not all owners have made their company their product. But many of those who have, have done so at the expense of their current profit potential, sacrificing this for higher capital valuations. We've seen this trend increasing over the past 20 years, with future performance playing a bigger and bigger role in equity valuations. On the margins, metrics like size or growth rate of the customer base started to produce more returns via an increase in capital valuation than any revenue those very customers could or would ever generate directly with the company's offerings.

Oftentimes, these strategies also resulted in a shift in customer expectations. We've all seen one of our competitors give away for free, or at least at a severe discount, some of the same features, knowledge, or value that historically made up a part of our base revenue. You can even find this happening in some commodities,[*] leading to models like freemium becoming commonplace. With freemium pricing (think of virtually any "free" app you use, from Zoom to LinkedIn), the company gives away basic features of its product to attract a wide customer base, only to capture a single-digit percentage of customers that are willing to pay for the premium features (3 to 5 percent typical goal with 1 to 2 percent average conversion in reality).

Other strategies that shifted customer expectations include Lyft using investor funding to subsidize below-cost rides in a battle with Uber for early market share. Or the infamous Casper, the direct-to-consumer mattress company that spent 75 percent of all gross earnings on inorganic customer acquisition—requiring investors to fund an operating loss of around $200 per unit sold.

Like a rogue wave, these "company as a product" strategies cut across the competitive landscape, shifting customer expectations in some of the bluest of oceans. But now, after years of continuous swell from optimizing for growth in the capital markets, many companies have been priced with expectations to deliver flawless performance and perfect value capture of their actual offerings.[†]

Over the past decade, we've sat with dozens of Fortune 500 executives as they evaluated and made tough choices for the future. We've observed a noteworthy drift firsthand in recent years, in many cases to these leaders' own chagrin and their companies' detriment. Leaders are spending less and less bandwidth scouting new passages to secure the fundamentals of their products and services and more on steering back and forth to keep up with endless external expectations and internal performance indicators.

In other words, there is a pull to spend too much time managing perceptions and messaging that affect near-term capital evaluations and not enough time developing and ensuring the success of their long-term core offerings. This plays out as either attempting to satisfy an

---

[*] OPEC intentionally flooded the market with oil and gas production in 2014, bankrupting many of their competitors and de-incentivizing half a decade of upstream investment.

[†] As of writing.

unrealistically broad stakeholder base or trying to avoid being seen as the one who got it wrong through the lens of historical hindsight.

As a result, we see a multitude of incoherent product strategies being pursued simultaneously. In the worst cases, we've seen companies knowingly head toward an inconvenient cliff in their business model without fomenting sufficient action among the larger team to correct their course. In previous decades, these "destined to fail" unit economics would have already been exposed, but as we write this book, many of these flaws are still being masked by the rising tide of capital valuations.

Tides cannot rise indefinitely. Sooner or later, receding waters will expose all the companies who have chosen to risk swimming naked. Some are already past the point of being able to change their fate. Unfortunately, even if your business didn't contribute to this situation, we'll all be faced with the same challenging environment when the tide finally does go out. Increasing the pricing power and profit margin of the value you already create will provide much-needed buoyancy in turbulent times.

Now is always the time to get out in front, catch up from behind, or catch the next wave. No matter how well you manage your business, given time and market pressures, waves of narrowing budgets will inevitably come crashing down on us all, forcing restructuring. Re-Valuing will be critical.

Why Re-Value?

If you've ever built a business from scratch, you know the early days require intense prioritization. You have to identify the big rocks, the high-level bits, and get them right. If a business makes it past the startup stage, it's because its leaders are good at this part—or at least got lucky. As time goes on, you fill in the aggregate around those big rocks to strengthen and support them—keeping your advantage by getting in front of as many future risks as possible. Later, many of those medium-sized pieces of aggregate will become entire departments, each with its own subset of objectives and strategies to further enhance and calcify these supporting structures.

However, no business operates in a completely static, predictable environment. No matter how perfectly your offering matched the environment and buyers when it was formed, over time, the white-space between those three elements (buyers, environment, and offering) almost always emerges. This is where unmonetized value lives. Of course, you can and should meet these changes by continually improving your offering. But if you were to respond to every emerging trend with the required investment to fully capitalize on it, you would surely go bankrupt; not to mention that most of these "trends" will end up fizzling away into the annals of history. Unfortunately, the trends that truly disrupt an established business are usually only identified with hindsight.

Of course, we love the underdog stories when only a few people saw the disruption coming. And indeed, there are rightfully cautionary tales of calcified incumbents who never even saw it at all. But it's easy to be seduced into concluding that all things are predictable, ignoring the dynamic nature of the environment in which we conduct business (McRaney 2013). Media has a tendency to put a microphone in front of the person who predicted the current outcome and often ignore the fact that they've been making that same prediction their entire career before getting it right.

In our experience, it's not a failure to be unable to predict the future. It's only a failure to not Re-Value your business at the moment a new future becomes predictable.

Opportunity and Overview

If not us, who? If not now, when?

—John F. Kennedy

Whether you own a company, manage a product team, or are simply a productive individual looking for an edge, how well you monetize the value you create has an outsized impact on your bottom line. In this context, monetizing means maximizing what people are willing to pay for the value you create. When we suggest you could double your earnings by making minor refinements to your existing operations, you should be skeptical. However, if we were to list out all the things you do that generate value for others, put a dollar amount on what they receive, and compare this to the amount you charged, we generally see you generating more than five times the value you priced your offering at on average. In other words, you're operating with a 5:1 capture ratio, so achieving a monetization ratio of up to 5:2 may not be as difficult as you might first think.

We all give away value for free, and that's to be expected. Some are given as sales and marketing in hopes of acquiring new customers. Some are given because we enjoy helping others and want to go above and beyond or out of a sense of purpose for the things we believe in and care about. And some of us give away value in the pursuit of being known and recognized in our fields. There are many valid reasons to give value away, and the point isn't to pinch every theoretical penny generated. The point is to be deliberate about how you monetize the value you generate and with whom.

Throughout this book, we use the term *offering* to include any product or service, whether tangible or intangible. In this way, your offering is any value you generate that someone else is willing to pay for (including the offering of working for someone as an employee). The *worst* we've achieved for our portfolio companies was a doubling of revenue and a 50 percent increase in profit margin over 12 months. (Though it's true, we have the liberty of selecting the businesses we partner with.) With experience ranging from turning the tides on runaway expense growth and lost revenue on $45 billion joint ventures to the aggressive growth of small-cap companies, we currently see the most untapped potential in professional services, business to business (B2B) products, and digital offerings.

Although the experience from which this book was derived is industry-agnostic, it should be noted that consumer goods is one area we don't focus on.[‡] This book will likewise not attempt to provide a step-by-step pricing process for a product; there's plenty of well-codified information on that elsewhere. Nor will we try and provide a roadmap for developing a new offering; thanks to previous publications like *Blue Ocean Strategy* (Chan 2005) and *Purple Cow* (Godin 2003), many have a clear picture of where to aim for when building never-seen-before "remarkable" products. But this book will build on the central thread of those publications: Great offerings are created not by following others but by discovering your own path.

Our focus is on all your product lines and services that already exist—those which you've worked hard to establish and are now generating value every day. Our goal is to spark insights that will help you monetize more of this value. To achieve this, we take the liberty of optimizing the entire offering cycle, from better identifying who gets the most value from your offering to gaining insights into how you position and package for maximum sales, through to identifying small refinements to how you reliably create and deliver this value as part of your operations.

Overview

This monograph dives into how humans assess the value of things. There are five sections. Each section offers a distinct yet complementary vantage aimed to unlock major potential for optimizing your earnings.

We open with a survey of Worthwhile Obstacles that often block people's efforts to improve their pricing power. Whether it's false positives that have people prematurely conclude they can't charge any more or a magnetic pull to follow well-recognized strategies at the

---

[‡]Nonetheless, we hope our friends at companies like Unilever will find the perspectives thought-provoking and applicable at the whole-company level.

cost of pricing yourself to the lowest common denominator, there's incredible value to be gained by being aware of common blockades to increasing your pricing.

In the next section, Atomic Behaviors, we will explore often-neglected variables that impact how your buyer makes their purchasing decision. We will help you maximize perceived value by identifying some optimal positioning for your offering. Then, we will share a way to map your customer's journey to maximize lifetime value. Lastly, we will introduce an innovative model that predicts how customers perceive and attribute value to what you offer. Collectively, you will discover new insights to increase how much people will pay for what you offer.

But insights often fail at implementation. Therefore, the fourth section of this book is on how to Re-Value reliably. We examine how your implementation strategies need to change based on your company's size, age, and expertise. Then, we introduce a simple and reliable framework designed to identify subtle adjustments to your business that yield the most significant returns, that is, how to Re-Value. Re-Value is conducted by aligning and optimizing the value your customers pay for across all your stakeholders in a way that is minimally disruptive.

To aid in the Re-Valuing of your offering, the final section shares the most valuable type of question we have ever come across to resolve competing priorities and potential objections. For example, a cynic could argue that raising prices is a disservice to customers, but the evidence tells a different story. We also include several true cases of Re-Valuing effectively and two cautionary tales where leaders ignored the principles we recommend. And to conclude, we will close out remaining threads explored throughout in the epilogue.

Thank you for investing your time in reading this book. After all, when writing a book on value, one must confront the nature of time as our most worthwhile commodity. To get the maximum return on your investment, we suggest reading with a specific challenge you're currently navigating in mind. It will provide the necessary granularity and relevance required to try on the ideas, models, and theories presented and gain one or two takeaways for your own business.

As you read, you may agree or disagree with the various premises presented. Down the road, we're certain that we'll disagree with some ourselves. However, the juxtaposition between what's presented and your view of what you're dealing with offers an opportunity for valuable insight. This contrast creates a jolt of possibility to discover a path forward where previously you only saw impassable terrain.

Every business is unique, none more than yours. We're not writing this book to try and convince you of a set of answers. Instead, we hope to crystalize some of the insights we've gained over the years, helping you and ourselves eliminate constraints and prompt a better set of questions to navigate.

But in your situation, you're the only expert that matters. Others cannot purport to know what you should do—nor do they have to live with the consequences of getting it wrong. This is an inherent dilemma that all leaders face. Whether you're accountable for thousands of people or just yourself, the challenge of scouting and mapping out your journey ahead is yours alone.

CHAPTER 2

Worthwhile Obstacles

The obstacle in the path becomes the path.

—Ryan Holiday

Over the past four decades, we've seen a shift in how companies manage their pricing. It has progressed from being a judgment call made by a small group of managers into a rather sophisticated evergreen practice aided by a team of specialists (Simon 2015). Now, in many large-cap companies we see an executive-level resource running a team of economists, focused on nothing but optimizing prices for incremental gains every day.

Often, the economist's progress of these teams is measured in basis points, so we're shocked by the returns brought about by fairly simple price optimization efforts, like the ones shared in this book, can create at companies who have not embraced this trend. Particularly noteworthy is the aggressively growing of small-cap companies. It can almost be like shooting fish in a barrel; they have enough of a customer base that there's solid data to be optimized, but they're small enough to pursue refinements that can double earnings with relatively little fanfare.

We are often surprised at how a majority of leaders neglect pricing, giving far more leadership bandwidth to things that don't produce as much long-term impact on their top and bottom line. Why do brilliant and effective leaders under-attend the price variable?

In some ways, it reminds us of the old innovator's dilemma (Christensen 1997). These leaders are not being ineffective; they're valuing the right things that are truly required to establish and grow their business. But in valuing these things, they don't attend to some key variables that allow for outsized returns. In this first section, we'll survey the most common obstacles we experience being in the way of a company optimizing its pricing. For some of them, the solution is as simple as knowing that these obstacles exist so you can sidestep them when they arise.

The Parable of Cash the Cow—Part I

Our Boy loved the time he spent on his grandfather's farm, but the thing he always looked forward to most was feeding the calves. The smallest one, a runt, quickly became his favorite. There was something special about this odd calf. She was the only all-black-haired dairy cow he'd ever seen. So, Our Boy named her Cash, after his grandfather's favorite singer, who always dressed in black.

Soon, Our Boy was stopping by the barn twice a day just to feed Cash and ensure that she kept growing well enough to stay part of the herd. The Grandfather, seeing this budding interest and looking to reinforce his grandson's dedication, made him an offer. He would give Cash to Our Boy, along with the old shed and pasture down by the road—everything he would need to run his own small farm. But Our Boy would have to pay the expenses, learn to run his mini-farm, and make his own financial decisions. And though he was still young he would have to attend some business classes at the local university. As The Grandfather had said many times, gone were the days when you could keep a farm running just by being a farmer. The threat of having to sell to a developer was being felt more and more; in fact, the sprawl from town had recently engulfed two of their neighbors.

Our Boy was ecstatic at the idea of taking care of Cash and helping more on the farm. This was something he could see himself doing for the rest of his life. But he was afraid to say yes. His grandfather was known as the best dairy breeder in the state, but Our Boy had seen the toll this work had taken on him: the long nights looking over bills and bank statements and the concerned calls over the weekend just to make sure there'd be enough supplies for the next week. The weight of the responsibility seemed too much, and Our Boy didn't think he was even old enough to know if this was what he wanted.

A little sad at the prospect of disappointing his grandfather, Our Boy was kicking dirt as he walked along one of the neighboring fencerows. The neighbor, old, blind, and retired from years of running the shop in town, could hear the weight of the world on Our Boy's shoulders as he walked by. "What's gnawing on you, young man?" he called out.

Our Boy walked up to the fence and explained the situation. "There's not much to business," the neighbor told him. "Keep it simple. Find what your customers pay for and offer it to them better than anyone else.

Your grandfather has the heart of an angel, but by trying to take care of everyone, he forgets who pays his bills, who keeps the farm running. That's why he's having to sell off the back forty, just to stay up to date with the Tax Man."

This was the first time he'd heard that his grandfather was selling land again. Our Boy remembered that he'd done it 5 years before, right after Our Boy's parents passed away and he came here to live. Always fast at math, he quickly realized if this continued, the whole farm would be gone by the time he reached his grandfather's age.

As the neighbor walked away, he murmured, "It seems like the most profitable thing you can do with an acre of land nowadays is sell it...."

Realizing he was still in earshot of Our Boy, he turned back and added, "...But remember, it's a crop you only get to harvest once."

That night, Our Boy told his grandfather he would accept the offer. And for the next few weeks, he spent every waking moment preparing the lower barn for Cash to move down. When he brought her down for the first time, she nudged his side with her head in gratitude. No longer pouring Cash's milk in the cooling vat with all the others, he tasted it straight for the first time. It was the best, most velvety smooth, perfectly balanced milk he'd ever had.

For the first time, Our Boy became eager to start taking business classes. He would figure out the best ways to sell Cash's milk so others could enjoy it too. One of his classmates told Our Boy how great his direct-to-customer sales business was, so Our Boy decided to set up a little stand by the road. But only one person stopped all day, and they were just asking for directions.

When another classmate mentioned the importance of marketing, Our Boy entered Cash's milk into the county fair and won the blue ribbon! Finally, his roadside stand enjoyed a small but steady stream of customers. However, handling this cut into the limited time he had to feed and milk Cash before and after school.

When he complained to the Little Girl from the farm next door about not having enough time, she offered to sell his milk for him at her vegetable stand. Our Boy was thrilled. But when she gave him the whole amount she'd earned for him on the first day, he handed half of it back to her. Now *she* was thrilled.

As the Little Girl took care of his customers, Our Boy took care of Cash. And now he had time to explore additional ways to build his mini business. He even started contemplating what would scale to the whole farm, hoping to eliminate his grandfather's stress and frequent sleepless nights worrying about its future. The Little Girl told him that a lot of customers were asking if they made butter. He remembered the words of his neighbor and hired the local baker to churn and whip a little every weekend for his regulars in exchange for keeping a third for himself. With the addition of a second product, Our Boy's budding business garnered the attention of his professor, who introduced him to a series of advisers who might be able to help him further.

First came a smooth-talking French salesman dressed in a suit and tie. He presented a dazzling array of slides, each bursting with more chevrons than the previous. He laid out a path forward and promised profitability in artisan cheese. All Our Boy had to do was supply the milk and sign the loan, and the man's company would handle the rest.

Then came the buttoned-up consultant wearing coke bottle glasses. This man didn't present anything; he just asked detailed questions about everything. When Our Boy didn't have an answer, he would shake his head and jot another line in his ledger. In the end, he wrote two numbers on a piece of paper: the first was how much money Our Boy's current business was losing out on, and the second was how much he could save even after paying his consultancy for their service. While Our Boy didn't like this consultant much, it seemed like it would be better to have him on his team than to not have him at all. So he passed on taking on the loan required for the cheese, but said yes to the consultant who could help him save more of what he made.

The final adviser was the one Our Boy was most eager to speak with. An ex-CEO of a dairy farm dressed in a clean pair of coveralls, he was promoting a new scientific breakthrough in blending milk. Our Boy was excited to have the guidance of someone who had faced what he was facing. But if the technology was so good, he wondered why this CEO never used it himself back when he was running his own farm. But Our Boy gladly gave the man milk samples from Cash and all the other cows, and when the ex-CEO returned with his scientist, they presented a secret formula for blending all the milk on the farm to taste just like Cash's.

Our Boy spent countless nights over the next few weeks putting together plans and packets, until finally he had a proposal he felt good about. He timidly shared it with his professor first and was relieved when it received the nod of approval. So they presented it together to his grandfather. Our Boy said it would take about 2 years, but in the end, they would be fully incorporated and operating with a lean but predictable profit. The Grandfather, seeing the pride in the professor's eyes at what his student had come up with, said yes.

By the time Our Boy graduated from school, he was the CEO of the largest company in town, and the third largest dairy farm in the state. Convinced that the farm was in good hands, The Grandfather signed over the final papers and moved back up the mountain to the little cabin on the mountain where he'd lived with his wife when they first got married. As success begets success, Our Boy rarely had the time to spend with Cash, or even much on the farm at all. He was often on the road to secure the next distribution deal or to follow a lead for the next herd acquisition, based on what they needed in their ever-expanding blending profile.

Our Boy followed many of the practices his grandfather had taught him. For example, in his pursuit to breed award-winning dairy cows, he would never consider buying someone else's grand champion. Grand champions were customarily auctioned off at the show after winning. Instead, he would jot down the name of the first runner-up and then drive to their farm a week later with his trailer, offering the farmer one or two bills above what they could get at the market—which they were almost always thrilled to accept. Of course, he would always sell his own grand champions, as they would go for two to three times what he could get for them at the market.

Years ago, Our Boy asked his grandfather why he did this. "Wouldn't you want the best cow, not the second best?" The Grandfather chuckled and pointed out that the difference between a grand champion and a first runner-up often comes down to one opinion at one moment in time. "At this level, whether or not the judge's bacon was burned that morning can have more impact on who wins than anything two farmers can compete for."

The more the farm grew, the more Our Boy was praised. After he sold public shares of the holding company he'd built for all the divisions and assets he now oversaw, the praise increased. His old professor even invited him to be interviewed at a dinner at the economics club in honor of his newest valuation. While these events gave him a spark of energy, he noticed that it didn't last as long as it used to when he was just trying to save his grandfather's farm. Now it seemed as if he spent more and more time capturing smaller and smaller increases in his profit margin.

As a way to contribute and give back, he invited the professor's current students to his next pitch day, where the students could join other companies and employees as they proposed business expansion ideas to Our Boy and his leadership team.

As pitches were hurled one after another, Our Boy started to realize he was less and less enthusiastic about the future. Just a few years before, who would have thought that he would be sitting there listening to a group of foreign delegates, who traveled all the way from their home country, just to learn from him and pitch him an overseas licensing partnership. But as they talked through their slides, Our Boy glanced out the window and caught sight of Cash, standing in the shade behind the brand new barn he'd built for her. He recognized the exhaustion in her too and suddenly wondered if it was time to sell. With the big payday, he could buy another farm and go back to milking a few cows and tending to the land a little each day. The Little Girl now had a small store in town, and he was certain that she'd still be happy to sell whatever he produced.

He knew, however, that he couldn't sell the farm and keep Cash; she was too much of a core asset to separate out. And even if he bought a new farm, it wouldn't be the farm his family had built. As he daydreamed about other ways to simplify, every possibility spun like merry-go-rounds of circular logic; everything was so interconnected, and any move he could take would result in someone who made the farm their home losing out. But if he didn't make a choice, he would be choosing to take the path he was currently on. And he knew he didn't want more of that. It was strange, he thought, thinking of selling everything just so he could go back to what he used to have. Now, though, with the confidence of experience, and the security of capital, a small farm was so much more attractive than it had ever been before.

As the pitch day wrapped up, Our Boy snapped back into CEO mode. He thanked everyone for their contributions and gave some words on how critical the creative thinking exhibited today was for the future of the company and their community at large. Turning to his inner team after the guest presenters said their final goodbyes, he announced that he would be unreachable over the long weekend everything they needed from him by the end of the day.

He knew where he had to go: up the mountain. It was funny, he mused; the older Our Boy got, the wiser his grandfather became.

To be continued...

Don't Slip on the Monetization Curve

If money is your hope for independence, you will never have it. The only real security that a man can have in this world is a reserve of knowledge, experience, and ability.

—Henry Ford

When you build a business, you progress through a set of well-recognized stages. Or if you run an existing business, you're managing the life cycle stages for at least one product. How well you navigate each of these stages will materially shape the pricing potential of your offering.

Whether you've discovered an unmet need in the market or you're just hanging your own shingle to continue the same work you've been doing for years, everyone goes through the phase of attracting their initial customers. This stage is best described as **Emergent**. As you create your offering and share it with others, you hope to get an encouraging reception—or at the very least some self-affirmation that there's something worth pursuing further and that people will indeed pay for it. This stage can be exciting and nerve-racking, and once solidified, your proven market may still be small, but the fond memories of this phase can last a lifetime.

After things get up and running, you begin testing variations to your offering and target market, validating your initial assumptions and exploring others in pursuit of additional market potential. In this stage of **Dynamic** exploration, you embrace deviations within your offering and explore with customers to discover what might be better received. You double down in areas where you see good results and retreat from the ideas that don't pan out. As your market expands, so does your confidence in your potential. After all, it's much more efficient to test and get feedback at this scale than later when you're ten times the size. As a particular customer base rises to the top, so do your efforts to establish a place with them.

This leads to the third stage where you focus on getting your offering **Embedded** among the most valuable customers in your now-proven market. This could take the form of securing a distribution deal, becoming a preferred vendor, or becoming the product of choice among

The Monetization Curve

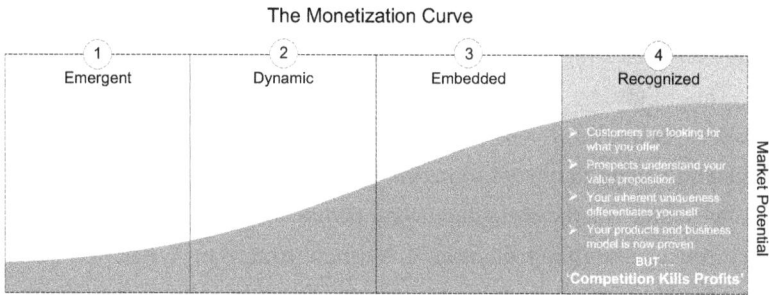

Figure 2.1 *Market potential of the monetization curve*

a niche subculture. Embedding your offering effectively will anchor your revenue, enable forward-looking investments, and help secure your position for years to come.

Effective navigation through the first three stages will bring you to the final stage of being **Recognized**. This is the enviable stage where people know your offering and ask for it by name. Your inherent uniqueness differentiates you from your competitors. Your offering is now fully proven beyond any reasonable doubt. You're recognized as a leader. You're recognized as the incumbent.

But when we look at the four stages from the vantage of monetization as illustrated in Figure 2.1, Stage 4 often doesn't look so desirable. With recognition comes increased competition. When your prospects ask for what you offer, they also ask for it from your competitors, who start to produce their own variants. Your competition increases, and competition kills profits.

For select offerings and industries, recognition and market domination will create significant barriers to entry of their competitors. This is particularly true in some industries with high sunk costs or significant intellectual property barriers. But for the overwhelming majority, as Peter Thiel declared in a 2014 lecture at Stanford, "Competition is for losers." Everyone loses profit margin regardless of who ends up with the larger market share.

From a monetization perspective, we don't see these stages as a linear progression but as worthy destinations in and of themselves. Each stage carries its own potential value for capture that's not available in any other stage. However, a warning for most companies, we find that there's often a magnetic pull to the recognition found in Stage 4; after all, so many business strategy examples are for companies in this stage.

This might be an unintentional by-product of sharing real-world business examples. If you want to communicate an example, it saves time and energy to choose something most people will be familiar with. So by talking all the time about companies we all recognize, we get a very real oversampling of Stage 4 business strategies. When you hold something up as an example, people tacitly infer value and are more likely to embrace it later simply because they have familiarity with it (Cytryn 2001). What gets praised gets emulated, even when it's not actually best for your business.

Fortunately, business experts are starting to advocate avoiding the competition that comes with Stage 4. There's a growing body of work in praise of staying in Stage 3; whether it's Warren Buffett's idea of the moat or *Zero to One*'s (Thiel 2014) provocation to create your monopoly, both point to and highlight the value of staying in the Embedded stage. Find your niche and then dig into a well-fortified position where others can't enter your market. It strikes a beautiful balance between maintaining a large market and building strong pricing power within it. However, we assert that there's even stronger pricing power in the earlier two stages, as illustrated in Figure 2.2. Whether or not that increased

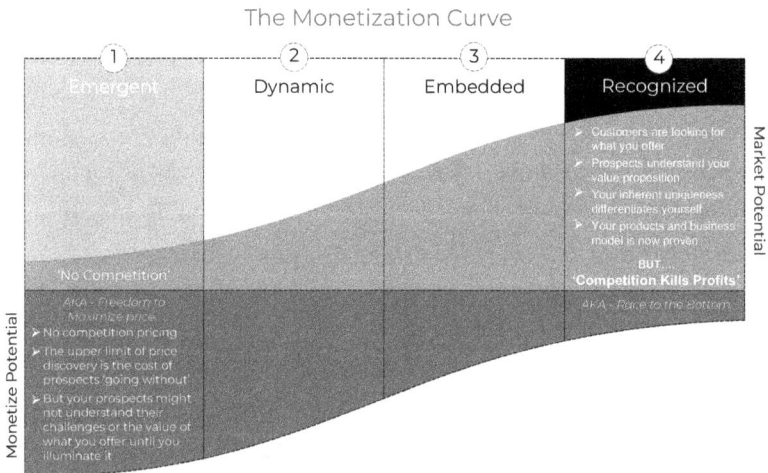

Figure 2.2 Monetize potential of the monetization curve

pricing power is worth the smaller market is something to be calculated for your specific offering.

Emergence can be one of our favorite stages when it comes to monetization potential because you're solving problems or opening up opportunities that your buyer probably doesn't even know they have. The downside is that nobody is actively looking for what you sell. But they will recognize the challenge your offering solves or the potential it enables once you point it out to them. Because of this, it often requires more skill and discipline on the sales front.

People outside of your ideal customer profile may never "get it." So, you must be diligent about discerning the difference between the value you offer for those who actually buy versus all the other potential value propositions that other stakeholders—and nonbuyers—may respond more favorably to. But the reward is the freedom to maximize the price on the value your customers receive. And the only competition you have is that they continue living without your offering.

Many people assume that to operate in the Emergent stage they must develop a never-seen-before product. This isn't necessarily required. It can be a well-recognized offering honed to address an emerging challenge or a long-forgotten discipline providing untapped value or insight for the current era. Often these are some of the most effective approaches, as you can leverage years of experience and quickly port it into a new market.

The point is to determine your most valuable position on the curve and fight against all the undercurrents that try to pull you away from there.

Executive Conclusion

Embrace Your Place on the Monetization Curve

This brief model challenges traditional thinking that associates your success with becoming a recognized leader in the market. Be strategic about where you position your offering on this curve based on its unique characteristics and don't rush to reach the "Recognized" stage, as you will often contend with the potentially destructive competition that

The Monetization Curve

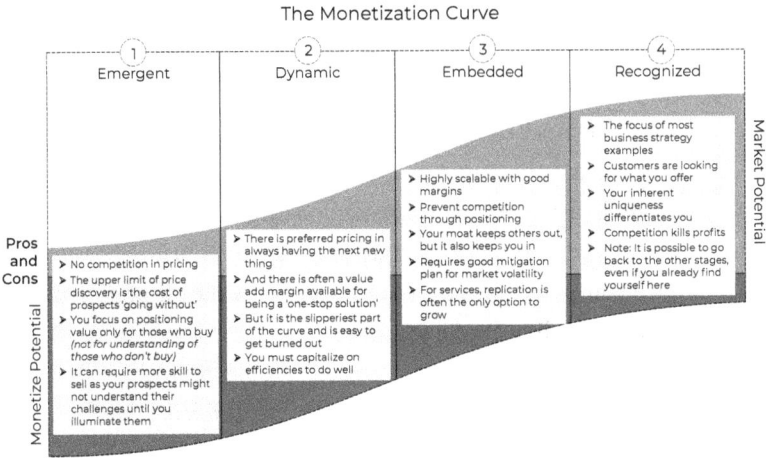

	1 Emergent	2 Dynamic	3 Embedded	4 Recognized
Pros and Cons	➤ No competition in pricing ➤ The upper limit of price discovery is the cost of prospects 'going without' ➤ You focus on positioning value only for those who buy *(not for understanding of those who don't buy)* ➤ It can require more skill to sell as your prospects might not understand their challenges until you illuminate them	➤ There is preferred pricing in always having the next new thing ➤ And there is often a value add margin available for being a 'one-stop solution' ➤ But it is the slipperiest part of the curve and is easy to get burned out ➤ You must capitalize on efficiencies to do well	➤ Highly scalable with good margins ➤ Prevent competition through positioning ➤ Your moat keeps others out, but it also keeps you in ➤ Requires good mitigation plan for market volatility ➤ For services, replication is often the only option to grow	➤ The focus of most business strategy examples ➤ Customers are looking for what you offer ➤ Your inherent uniqueness differentiates you ➤ Competition kills profits ➤ Note: It is possible to go back to the other stages, even if you already find yourself here

Figure 2.3 Pros and cons of the monetization curve

comes with it. One stage isn't inherently better than any other. From a monetization perspective, treat Emergent, Dynamic, Embedded, and Recognized as independent destinations.

Any of the stages can be a rightful place to call home, as illustrated in Figure 2.3, each with its own set of rules to optimize your monetization rate.

Avoid Pricing Riptides

Experience is the hardest kind of teacher.
It gives you the test first and the lesson afterward.

—Oscar Wilde

Over the past 5 years, 351 people have died in the United States because they swam against a riptide and drowned (NOAA 2022). By comparison, less than 30 people have died from shark attacks in the past 50 years (Florida Museum of Natural History 2022).[*] Riptides are overlooked killers, but they're also convenient. Surfers paddle out on the riptide every day to get to the lineup and catch their next wave. Like the moving sidewalk at the airport, they take them out quicker. Being caught in a riptide unknowingly can wear you out and cause you to drown. But if you know where they exist and how they affect you, you can use them to your advantage to get where you want to go faster.

The following is a set of *pricing riptides* that affect how people will value your offering. Like riptides in the ocean, we often see people unintentionally get caught fighting them, then prematurely conclude that they've maxed out the pricing power of their offering. While it may be too early to call these laws, in our experience, we've found them reliable enough to no longer spend our time and effort fighting them. Instead, like the surfer, we paddle straight into them and plan our pricing strategies accordingly.

Riptide #1

You don't deliver equal value to all your customers.

Many people are so motivated to bring in the widest possible customer base that they end up pricing themselves to the lowest common denominator. We often see companies position their offering to try and lead to the greatest number of sales, to the most prospects. But this often results in the worst monetization ratio for the value they generate.

---

[*]Unprovoked shark attacks off the shores of the United States that led to fatalities, and exploratory bites are more frequent.

In many companies we worked with, doubling profit margin *while* increasing total revenue involved the narrowing of target customers and, in a few cases, firing existing customers that weren't a match for the value they created (particularly with service firms).

Now more than ever, having an offering tailored "for someone like me" or "in my situation" is reaping outsized rewards. The value you generate for your customers isn't the same for all of them, so be careful not to price to the lowest common denominator. Find those who will pay more for your offering and double down on your efforts to reliably deliver it to them.

Riptide #2

Your prospects don't value a better product as much as you do.

(If they did, they would be your competition, not your customer.)

They say if the only tool you have is a hammer, you tend to see every problem as a nail. But as it turns out, often it's the person who lives in a world full of nails that is the only one motivated enough to invent the very first hammer.

Venture capitalists have long given preference to founders who are building a product that solves an unmet need the founders themselves have. This helps the venture capitalists avoid investing in someone who doesn't have implicit knowledge of their intended customer base. However, it does not close the gap completely. When working with founding owners in particular, we often see them so excited to share about what they offer, how it works, or what it will do for you that they unknowingly give away the very knowledge that makes their offering valuable.

It would be akin to Coke being so happy to share the value of their sweet refreshing drink that they told people the recipe so they could appreciate the brilliance of it for themselves. This can result in one of two undesirable situations: either the prospect concludes they don't like that solution before giving it a try or they like it, but now they know what they need to make it themselves and start looking to source the ingredients elsewhere at a lower cost.

These founders have enough shared interest with their prospect that they can discuss their solution for hours—without realizing that they're pursuing two very different aims. [For clarity, we're not suggesting you shouldn't give away value before a sale. Nor do we advocate giving everything away and expecting that good things will come back. Both can work, but both have limitations and trade-offs.] Our point is to be careful not to collapse what motivates you to build a better solution with what motivates your most valuable customers to buy it.

Riptide #3

What people say they value is different from what's embodied in their buying decisions.

No matter how much encouragement or praise is provided in customer feedback, there are only two metrics we've ever found that indicate the type of value reliable enough to optimize how much you can charge: time and money. First, is a person willing to spend their time exploring your offering? Note that this is not time chatting with your salesperson or time spent drinking your alcohol at a conference happy hour. This is time focused on thinking through and envisioning the application of your offering in their day-to-day life. Second, is a person willing to spend money to give your offering a try? In short, if you want to know what a person will pay for, pay close attention to how they spend their time and money. Buyers can readily recite a set of explicit justifications for their purchase decision but rarely can they utter any implicit meaning that truly motivated them to buy or not.

As Malcolm Gladwell so poetically put it in his speech on "Choice, happiness and spaghetti sauce," (2004)

> *People don't know what they want! As Howard [Moskowitz; an American market researcher and psychophysicist] loves to say, "The mind knows not what the tongue wants." It's a mystery! And a critically important step in understanding our own desires and tastes*

is to realize that we cannot always explain what we want, deep down. If I asked all of you, for example, in this room, what you want in a coffee, you know what you'd say?

Every one of you would say, "I want a dark, rich, hearty roast." It's what people always say when you ask them. "What do you like?" "Dark, rich, hearty roast!" What percentage of you actually like a dark, rich, hearty roast?

According to Howard, somewhere between 25 and 27 percent of you. Most of you like milky, weak coffee. But you will never, ever say to someone who asks you what you want that "I want a milky, weak coffee."

By attending to what your prime buyer spends their time and money on, you can begin to infer and extrapolate the values they embody and then optimize your offering to match. This also aids in calibrating any price complaints you receive that may or may not infer cost tolerance. After all, there are people who will make negative comments about your price whether you charge full price, three times the price, or 50 percent off.

Riptide #4

Your prospects don't care about your offering, they care about what it affords them.

We often see owners get slightly dismayed by the criteria that others use to judge their offering. Buyers will always use a set of *heuristics* to judge what you offer. Heuristics are the everyday rules of thumb and mental shortcuts we use to make decisions. They're not guaranteed to be optimal, perfect, or even rational. But they're generally sufficient for reaching an immediate goal. Fundamentally, people spend their time and resources on what they perceive will get them closer to a place they value more. As Harvard professor Theodore Levitt famously put it back in the 1960s, "People don't want to buy a quarter-inch drill, they want a quarter-inch hole."

People rarely pursue what they really want directly; instead, they pursue that what they've already concluded, or experienced, will get them closer to the goal or instantiation that embodies what they value. In this way, when they buy, your offering is only ever an instrument to progress closer to where they want to be. What one will pay for will always make perfect sense from this vantage. We have yet to discover a person who intentionally buys an inferior product or chooses to throw away their money. Instead, we find they're choosing the most viable pathway they see available at the time. We know we've found that pathway when we can envision doing the same ourselves. Increasing pricing power is about repositioning your offering in a higher valued place along that path.

Riptide #5

Your offering will commodify with time, but your profit margin doesn't have to.

To put the first part of this statement in human terms, everybody gets old. But how many people do you know who are still fighting the aging process? For example, when someone older than 65 wears skinny jeans, often it doesn't make them look younger so much as accentuate their age—drawing a contrast.[†] With your offering, the goal is not to stop from growing old but to ensure to age gracefully. Most are familiar with what happens over time to the other offerings in their respective fields.

For example, the moment a company celebrates the win of becoming a preferred vendor to a very large corporation is the same moment they can start the countdown clock until they get their annual pricing haircut by the procurement department. With the head start of knowing and accepting, not resisting, the next stage in aging, you can invest in an offensive position to maintain or even improve your monetization ratio for that next stage of the product life cycle.

[†]No offense if you're the exception to this rule of thumb; if that is the case, we're honored that Keith Richards is reading this book.

Riptide #6

Your price is not just a number, it is a signal.

What does your pricing signal about you? Pricing has a dual role in business: it will determine your revenue, and it signals your value. Businesses can use price as a tool to position their offerings within the market, signal the level of quality or value the offering delivers, and attract their right kind of customers.

For example, you may choose to price so aggressively you deliver a dopamine hit to the type of buyers looking to score a deal, who in turn provide you with free marketing to the fellow members of their value hunting tribe. In these cases, you can move a disproportionally amount of inventory (or penetrate a market faster) than traditionally expected on your supply and demand curve simply by signaling "a good deal," a la the Costco Effect.

Or a higher price may deter price-sensitive customers but attract those seeking premium products or services. But be forewarned, as the price increases, not only does the expectation of quality but also the level of disgust and backlash for any misstep in failing to meet those expectations (Gneezy et al. 2014).

Riptide #7

Your past pricing creates future expectations… but your future isn't written yet.

The pricing decisions you have already made create hidden expectations in your customers' minds about what they'll pay in the future. This is especially the case if you've been consistent in your pricing strategy over a long period of time. Any drastic changes in pricing can be met with resistance or even backlash from your customer base. It's crucial to navigate them wisely when contemplating price changes.

However, far more often we see too many leaders make the mistake of being too constrained and overly limited by this concern without any evidence that they should. Or they assume they must give up their current customer base for one that would be willing to pay more. Too often people are so afraid of negative pushback, they have never even run one test case to validate their concerns and then proceed with certainty with the same old scenario they are familiar with, leaving money on the table.

While we often recommend timing a new price strategy with a major version update or refinement to your product, in our experience, it is always worth exploring beyond a reasonable doubt, how do we truly know our customers won't pay more?

Executive Conclusion

Ride your Riptides

There are a lot of variables that affect how people perceive your offering, and many can be optimized to improve your pricing power. But there are some you can't control. Without discernment, it's easy to be caught swimming against the current and wasting what could otherwise be profit trying to impact the wrong ones.

- The value that your product or service offers is not uniform across all customers, and there is a divergence between why you value your offering and why they value it.
- Overexplaining your product or service might inadvertently undermine its perceived value.
- Compliments feel great, but they don't cost much for people to give.
- Never resist the "rules of thumb" or mental shortcuts your prospects use to judge what you offer.
- The best indicators of what a person truly values lie in where they already spend their time and money.

Buyers are always more interested in the benefits your offering affords them than your offering itself. Positioning your offering in a manner that clearly registers for your buyer as bringing them closer to where they value being is often more effective. But to achieve this, understanding what motivates buying behavior becomes critical. How do you predict what a person is willing to spend their time and money on in advance?

CHAPTER 3

Atomic Behaviors

Never forget the 6-foot-tall man who drowned crossing the stream that was 5 feet deep on average.

—Howard Marks

It is often easier to think about valuing your offerings in terms of markets, aggregating and averaging the individuals that do the buying. The problem is that this smooths out natural variations that hide opportunities and obstacles to optimizing what actual customers are willing to pay. To improve your pricing power, you need to know what a specific individual is willing to pay for your offering. As the American self-made billionaire Sam Zell reminds his team, "We don't buy markets, we buy deals." Buying is idiosyncratic.

Buying is also an emotional decision, technically speaking, made by our limbic system (Damasio 1994). The limbic system is the part of our brain involved in processing emotions and is responsible for our behavior. If you ask an appraiser what something is worth, they'll utilize a set of explicit measurements and calculations—this work is done using the higher faculties of their neocortex. But if you ask if they would like to buy it themselves, they won't be able to answer without engaging their limbic system. And the limbic system processes information faster than the cognitive brain can handle explicit thinking, so it always has a head start. In our experience, most business to business (B2B) sales material does a great job of arming the buyer to justify and debate their decision with their colleagues but rarely offers anything better than a random chance at influencing their actual purchasing decision.

Your brain will use logic and rationality to justify and strengthen a decision after you've made it, but logic and rationality will not influence the decision in advance. After all, in day-to-day life, how many times have you successfully used logic and rationality to change the mind of your significant other when you're in disagreement? As Daniel Kahneman puts it,

> Subjectively, it feels like you believe in something because you have the arguments for it. That's not the way it works, it works the other way around. You believe in the conclusion, and then you create supporting arguments. That's fundamental. (UBS 2019)

So if logic, rationality, and objective modeling don't provide reliable insight into what a person is willing to pay for something, what does?

Historically, there have been too many variables when confronting an individual idiosyncratic buyer to ever try and model all of them, so most pricing approaches are often based on aggregating the behavior of individuals so that the relevant variables can rise to the top. Approaches like behavioral pricing proved valuable in accounting for narrower types and classifications of customers. But these approaches still had the same unknown variable challenge—meaning one could easily fit a model to the status quo based on the current weighing of the set of relevant variables. But when something in the environment changes, a previously irrelevant variable becomes active and requires a *post hoc* adjustment based on the actual outcome. It's the classic "map is not the territory" problem; after all, the cartographer must have seen the territory first in order to map its properties.

After seeing so many brilliant minds working from a top-down perspective during our careers about 15 years ago, we became curious about how much might be gained from a bottom-up approach. We began by looking for an underlying process that would allow us to isolate the variables at play and predict them in advance, individual by individual, only then to build up a predictive aggregate model. However, our aim has simply been to predict the upper bounds of what a given person would be willing to do or pay to achieve or acquire a given thing. Then we use this prediction to replicate, aggregate, and roll out new, more optimal offerings and pricing.

Very quickly, we felt like scientists looking for the subatomic structure. As you may recall, the entire periodic table and everything we see around us comprises the same three things: protons, neutrons, and electrons. It's the way they're combined that creates drastically different elements and properties. This line of thinking sparked our wonder on two things: first, is there something analogous in human decision making? And second, if so, would it allow for better prediction of buying behavior?

What Grips Your Attention?

If a cluttered desk is a sign of a cluttered mind,
of what, then, is an empty desk a sign?

—Albert Einstein

The human brain has a computational efficiency problem. While it only makes up 1 to 3 percent of your body's mass, it consumes 20 to 25 percent of your total energy. An infant human has to be born approximately three months earlier than the average mammal to accommodate its larger head size. Adding any more computational "hardware" would come at too large of a cost. So our brain gains additional efficiency through impressive "software" optimization in how it selects relevant inputs from the almost infinite data set that makes up our environment. We've evolved to become quite effective at realizing what's relevant to us at any given moment in order to take action based on our goals—by ignoring the great majority of everything around us. From a cognitive neuroscience point of view, John Vervaeke, PhD, at the University of Toronto has named this underlying physiological process "Relevance Realization" and describes its role as "the underpinning of cognition."

We assert in today's connected world, the challenge of effective marketing and sales is no longer simply getting in front of your ideal customers. The true challenge has shifted to more effectively interacting with the relevance realization of your most valuable buyers. After all, you don't ignore advertisements for a car you're thinking about buying. In fact, you typically get a rush of dopamine, the feel-good chemical, if it's a commercial you haven't seen before. And it's shocking when you notice how many people in your neighborhood seem to have just started driving that make and model of car, this might be the simplest example of relevance realization in action.

The following are principles that affect the relevance realization of buyers and impact how your offering gets perceived.

Positioning Beyond Problems

Asking, "What problem do you solve?" has become a popular way for investors and potential business partners to solve a problem they themselves face. When evaluating a company for investment, it's important to discern if the company has created a solution in response to an unmet need in the market or if the founders have become enamored by "a solution in search of a problem." The former allows for the effective analysis of market potential and stands on a firmer footing for the business case, while the latter is much more akin to funding scientific research. It could turn into something someday, but you're investing in speculation; it's a very different kind of investment requiring an even larger upside potential to fund the risk.

However, for all the benefits this popular question provides, its overuse can gloss over two other, more valuable pricing positions:

1. The embodiment of the desired destination itself.
2. A shortcut for getting to where your buyer wants to get to.

For example, it would be silly to consider the Four Seasons as solving a lodging problem. And it would take some unnecessary linguistic gymnastics to define them as a solution for how to spend one's leisure time. Like many luxury goods, the Four Seasons simply offers an embodiment of the destination itself. Whether it's a $2,000 handbag or a $400 bottle service, selling these objects and experiences *is actually a cost-effective way* to rent or own a piece of the destination their customers hope to reach someday. It might take another few decades—or even another lifetime—to be able to own a private villa with a full-time butler, but for one week a year, you can live as if you already do.

Selling a shortcut, or an alternative way to get your buyer to a higher-valued place they want to be, has unique pricing advantages as well. On one end of this continuum, a business to business customer may have a process with a well-defined number of steps, each with a quantifiable time and cost; it's easy to calculate how much value is brought by a new offering that reduces the number of steps and duration. It's also very easy to know in advance whom the offering will create value for,* and these types of offerings are often the ones well suited for case studies and demonstrations.

This holds with consumer products as well; the early iPhone ads didn't tell you about the features of the phone, they showed little vignettes of it being used in everyday life. Even with the original iPod, Apple's total addressable market wasn't defined by people who had the problem of carrying around binders full of CDs. But once they showed you could walk down the street with your entire music library in your pocket, they created a shortcut for people to have something they valued more with less effort, and customers happily paid for it.

On the other end of the continuum, away from quantifiable time and expense, is the potential for revolution, disruption by a new way of operating, or a technological breakthrough. This positioning taps into our well-known tendency to value the potential performance, *ex ante*, more than the proven performance of something we're already familiar with, *ex post*. There's a premium that comes from being the next new thing (Kahneman 2011). Many people will pay more for something that offers potential, even when it clearly eclipses their own verifiable bottom-up estimates of what they'll get out of it.

Side Note: In the early 2000s, the famous Moneyball strategy (Lewis 2004) is an example that leveraged the inverse of this principle to the advantage of smaller-budget baseball teams, which a variety of other businesses followed suit. Teams began to recognize that proven performance was being undervalued in the league and they could combine it in the aggregate to produce the desired outcome, dominating in a far more cost-effective way.

The Importance of Novelty

Being able to infer where your prime buyer is trying to get is important. But even more important is positioning your offering effectively. Your *salience landscape* is the way you determine relevance realization through

---

*Example, Monsanto, the agrochemical company, often bases their product development and prices on a 30 percent value capture for the "shortcut" they provide.

automated decisions about how to commit your attention. Your offering must sufficiently match your potential customer's salience landscape for them to ever even perceive it in the first place.

Here is where novelty becomes important. While novelty is commonly defined as the quality of being new, original, or unusual, it's worth noting that to be novel, it must first be recognized. To recognize it is to place it in a category of other things that already exist. This brings us back to not resisting the heuristics your buyer uses to evaluate your offering, as shared in Riptide #4. They'll put your offering in a category of things that already exist; it's up to you to help them decide which one.

New categories are created in hindsight, not by sheer marketing will. The more time a prospect spends exploring your offering, the higher-resolution picture they develop as part of their salience landscape, and the more they'll end up valuing it. The rarity and uniqueness of a sports car, piece of art, or custom-made product can attract people to explore it in greater detail, to covet and value acquiring it even more.

Novelty, of course, is ephemeral. There are many approaches, incentives, or offerings that will produce massive returns soon after they're introduced, only to have the effect wane and regress to the mean. That's not to say don't pursue them, but to orchestrate the journey over time to capture the gains and progress onto the next adjacent thing that will continue the value creation and capture. To stay on the "novel" edge that maximizes engagement, you'll need to let the way your offering is presented evolve along with your buyer's salience landscape.

The Expert Predicament

We often see companies unintentionally exclude a whole subset of their target market by advocating their solutions. While this does work on occasion, when analyzed in situ to their target market's salience landscape, it often looks a lot like preaching to the choir. The Expert <> Prospect relationship can be ironic when viewed bluntly from a distance:

1. A prospect seeks an expert's point of view for something they're uncertain how to deal with.

2. The prospect then assesses the validity of what the expert says and will only follow it *if* it matches their current experience of what they're facing.

3. But, if the expert saw the situation the same way the prospect does, they wouldn't be an expert at overcoming it.

FBI hostage negotiator Chris Voss was faced with this dilemma when negotiating for kidnapping victims on foreign soil where the United States had limited jurisdiction. With those stakes, he could not risk rejection and developed a systematic way to ensure his expertise would be utilized by the locals.

> *You don't have to establish rapport, you gotta establish competence. The relationship will come, but what people wanna know right off the bat is there any reason to think that you're competent?*
>
> *"I'm a hostage negotiator with the FBI." That will get me the next five seconds. Okay. Chris, he's a hostage negotiator. Maybe he knows what he's talking about. Which was really how are you gonna help me? Every single person, anybody who's selling, or in business, everybody you encounter, that's exactly what they ask themselves as soon as you start talking. How are you gonna help me? They might not be that explicit with it but as human beings, that's what we say.*
>
> *So the very next thing you gotta lay out is do you see the problem that they see. 'Cause their question is, do I gotta explain this to you? Bang, you take that right away by giving them a short quick version of what they're looking at without giving 'em any answers.* (Voss 2018)

Being able to describe the obstacle or opportunity a prospect faces and characterize the terrain they must navigate casts a far wider net than prematurely advocating a particular answer or strategy. If you prematurely advocate your solutions, you force people into a value judgment. Those who value your solutions already are often people who have already gained quite a bit of the benefit in doing so and thus are often coming to you to reinforce their experience—or to prophesize to other stakeholders who don't yet value it and thus won't pay for it.

The prospects who could have the most value unlocked, conversely, are those who have never even explored your solution as a viable option in any detail. They have never explored it because it doesn't sufficiently match their salience landscape and has not crossed the threshold of their relevance realization. If you force a value judgment too soon, prospects will often conclude your offering is "good for others" but is not "for them."

Something must have an emotional impact before it will attract enough attention to be explored and mapped in accordance with its sensory properties (Peterson 1999). This means we must have a connection with something already before we are willing to explore it. Too often, people resist the existing connection and the comparisons prospects make with what they offer. This is especially true of innovative products or new services people have not experienced before. Buyers are far more comfortable with what is familiar to them. But when your potential buyer's first impression is being told, "This isn't what you think it is," it often forces them onto the offramp of engaging with what you have to offer.

Telling someone that their initial perception is incorrect can create cognitive dissonance, where there is a discrepancy between what they believe and what they are being told. This is not to say you don't ever need to shift how people think about what you offer, but in order to shift it, let their existing connection serve as an anchor, then build and relate the new information to their existing knowledge.

The Red Herring of "Differentiation"

Often when a conversation migrates to what differentiates your offering from others, we immediately run into miscommunication and navel-gazing. There are a lot of backgrounds and contexts in which people ask this iconic question. For example, we could be seeking to understand very different things depending on who's doing the asking.

1. **Investors**—What do you own that others don't or can't? (i.e., Do you have a moat that will protect my investment from others copying you?)

2. **Prospects**—Tell me what I can only get by going with your offering. (I'll judge if that has any value to me.)
3. **Job Interviewer**—What is your unique but relevant skill for the job at hand?
4. **Press Interviewer**—Tell me something unexpectedly intriguing that might grab or keep my reader's attention.

There's a wide spectrum of intent contextually framed under this iconic question of "Differentiation," but when it comes to marketing your offering, Seth Godin may have put it best (2016):

"If you're talking about "differentiating yourself," you've started from the place of:

A: I define myself by my competition; how do I differentiate myself from them?

and

B: I'm in a commodity business.

Neither of those things is true if you start from the other place, which is what does that person, just that person, need? And what can I provide that only I can provide?

Seth calls attention to the same pitfall we introduced in the monetization curve, that is, pursuing recognition over one's strongest economic position. Admittedly, it does feel good to be asked "What differentiates you?" and to answer confidently. Maybe that's why so many of the people you pay to help you market and brand yourself still ask you for it—it makes you, their client, feel good. But when the goal is persuasion, it rarely meets the threshold of relevance realization for your customers. For example, when was the last time you cared what your banker thought made their bank different from others?

Executive Conclusion

People only perceive offerings that map to their existing salience landscape and take action on an offering when it crosses the threshold of their relevance realization.

The human brain is efficient at choosing relevant inputs from the environment based on our goals, which are simply instantiations of things we value. At the atomic behavior level, what you sell only ever falls into one of four positions:

1. A pathway to progress closer to where your customer wants to be.
2. A tool to overcome an obstacle in their way of making progress.
3. An embodiment of their motivating destination itself.
4. An obstacle in their way (most relevant to avoid in business to business offerings).

If it's not one of these, it doesn't even register for them at all.

For over two decades, targeted digital marketing proved incredibly potent and cost-effective. Now, because of that success and the fact that advertisements are sold to the highest bidder, some segments have seen their cost per click multiply several times over. The better you architect your offering as part of your prime buyer's relevance realization, the more organic sales increase and the less you will have to spend on customer acquisition.

Connecting with consumers on an emotional level and allowing them to relate the product or service to something they already understand can be a powerful way to gain their interest and engagement. As they become more invested, there is an opportunity to provide additional information and shape their understanding without alienating them by immediately contradicting their initial impressions.

In conclusion, people will pay for a solution to overcome a problem they have, but they may pay even more for a new approach, particularly when it offers the possibility of additional upside. And there's an even higher premium available for capture by selling the embodiment of your buyer's destination itself. Each of these positions has a different monetization range, and within each of these ranges, the monetization potential fluctuates at different points in time.

The Most Overlooked Pricing Variable

Isn't it funny how day by day nothing changes, but when you look back, everything is different?

—C.S. Lewis

In our experience, the most overlooked pricing variable is *time*.

Smaller obstacles on the five-yard line from your customer's goal can be worth more to resolve than larger obstacles on the 50. The closer your buyer is to achieving their motivating destination, the more they'll pay to overcome what's in their way. Remember Pricing Riptide #4: Your prospects don't care about your offering; they care about what it affords them.

You yourself have probably even said yes to something you acknowledged was a bit more expensive than you would ordinarily pay, simply because you didn't want to spend the time and energy it would take to go another route. Which swath of time you position your offering in affects your pricing power. In order to optimize the time dimension, we need to map your customer journey—from prospect to customer, from customer to customer alumni. The more deliberately and coherently you do this, the higher the monetization ratio you can achieve as part of the total customer life cycle.

Loss Leaders and Gatekeepers

When optimizing initial offerings, we tend to avoid *loss leader* strategies. In general, we prefer initial offerings to be priced with the highest margins. Particularly with service firms, we've seen company after company under-account for the total effort cost of onboarding a new customer.

Generally, acting on something for the first time requires reducing your initial goal sufficiently to take any new action toward it (Beck 2020). We often find that's the key to creating a good initial offering. Low risk doesn't mean low margin. New buyers often want to experience what you offer before committing to their top spend. But from there on, the pricing precedent you establish tends to become the expectation.

If you offer a discount, you could unintentionally be constituting your customer as a "sucker" if they fail to negotiate that same discount the next time they buy from you.

We also find the price of your initial offering is an important "gatekeeper" to your customer selection criterion—a structured way to ensure your buyer is willing to spend their time and money on the rest of what you have to offer.

In recreational overlanding, multiday 4×4 driving and camping adventures on unpaved roads and trails, there are obstacles at the start of a trail known as gatekeepers. The gatekeeper is a difficult situation you have to drive across at the very beginning. These gatekeepers could easily be eliminated during regular trail maintenance, but that's not the point; they are a deliberate hurdle to turn back drivers who don't have the vehicle or the skills for what will come further down the road when it is far more costly to try and turn back around.

Going forward with the wrong buyers can be worse for your bottom line than not booking the revenue altogether. Once you've discovered your strongest positioning and pricing power, there's a useful element of building the right-sized "gatekeeper" into your initial offering. This can ensure those who go past that point truly embody the values required to be mutually beneficial long-term customers.

Prospect to Customer

Is it better to educate your prospective buyers on the value you offer and what they should care about before you make your first sale? Or should you create your initial offering to do that so you can get paid for your time and expertise while doing so?

It depends—specifically, on your offering and the typical entry point of your prime buyer. The following are some common scenarios that will affect your decision:

- *Loss Avoidance*—Snatching victory out of the jaws of defeat will always be valued more than avoiding getting close to failure in the first place. Your potential value capture is increased any time your buyer's intended progress is stopped and at risk of being lost. Roughly speaking, the amount of negative emotion you experience from a $5,000 loss requires the positive emotion of a $10,000 gain to match (Kahneman and Tversky 1979).

- *Prevention*—Prevention of obstacles is generally valued at a level of magnitude less than resolving it once it's faced. While one may be willing to pay $10 million to resolve a current obstacle in the way of making $100 million, they're likely only willing to spend $1 million to prevent that obstacle from ever arising again. And this is assuming the challenge is well known and appreciated with limited options to overcome.

  We find the best time to sell proactive prevention is after solving a failure or near-failure. While one can rightfully scoff at this strategy—objectively, the buyer would be better off with prevention in advance—most prospects won't value the prevention offering enough to buy it proactively (unless it is required to achieve something else they want, for example, buying a cyber security audit—to get insurance required—to be able to be a qualified vendor—to sell to a large customer).

- *Insurance*—If your product is based on prevention, or on mitigation of an incident once it's occurred, the more *foreseeable* you can make what your offering avoids, the more it will be valued. Foreseeability is composed of two elements: first, the buyer's experience with it happening and second, the granularity of the picture they have in their mind's eye when thinking about it happening in their current situation.

  Surprisingly, the least important variables are the actual statistical likelihood of it happening and the quantifiable exposure cost in case it does. Note: we're not fans of the old 1920s FUD Factor sales technique (fear, uncertainty, and doubt). Our point here is to simply highlight the necessity of translating truly valuable insights and truths into a foreseeable format.

Customer Alumni

Most people appreciate the value of starting with the end in mind. But companies rarely pay enough attention to the point where a customer stops being an active customer. They don't think through and engineer the experience and value of past customers or "customer alumni."[†] Instead, they focus on maximizing customer acquisition or eliminating attrition altogether. But by doing this, they often unintentionally undermine their true value and total lifetime earnings.

For example, a patron of a restaurant will become a customer alumnus if they move out of town. But similar to a former graduate of a university, they can be incredibly valuable to the customer cycle. While they won't be making donations, they are very likely to invite friends to eat there every time they go back—or to longingly recommend the place to others who now live close by.

When you leave your past customers with a meaningful way to share your offer with others, you create a positive feedback loop in your customer's journey. However, when companies hastily add suboptimal offerings to try and retain customers, rather than building a thoughtful transition strategy that maximizes total value capture, they end up degrading the quality, goodwill, and nostalgia for what created the most value in the first place.

An interesting example of someone we all know who did this well was Jerry Seinfeld, with the way he managed and ended his namesake TV show. During the ninth and final season, the show was so successful among his customer base that he had to turn down an offer of $115 million, $5 million an episode, for a 10th season. Instead, he left the audience wanting more—and effectively transitioned them to getting more through syndication, DVD, and now streaming—as a minority of the total audience of the ninth season had ever watched seasons one through three.

[†]Note that when we say customer alumni, we're not implying they'll never buy from you again, only that they've gone through the customer cycle and exited on the other side of what you offer (for now).

This decision wasn't made in a vacuum; it formed part of a deliberate strategy that shaped the show from the start. By asking from day one how they could maximize the value of their show, the producers bucked the trend of including timely plot lines and commentary on current events, or using misunderstandings caused by new technology for comic effect. As a matter of fact, with the exception of telephones or the glow from a TV (note, not even the TV itself), you rarely saw anything that would speed up the dating of the show.[‡]

Obviously, there's little that can be done with clothes, cars, and hairstyles. But with most things under their control, the writers focused on the mundane, universal things audiences decades in the future are still able to relate to. Such small refinements starting on day one led to each of the two creators earning more than $400 million per five-year syndication cycle, even 30 years later.

Executive Conclusion

Monetize Your Customer Journey Over Time

When you lay out your whole customer journey through your offerings, you can optimize how time affects the value of what you offer and maximize the value capture at every phase. The first thing we do when thinking about working with a new company is to create a four-dimensional price map. The first three dimensions highlight opportunities in each of the traditional pricing models, *cost, competitive, and value*—and we almost always find some low-hanging fruit just in benchmarking these three. But it's when we place the buyer's journey in time, a breakthrough in monetization often jumps out.

As you highlight and extend out into the future what your customer ultimately hopes to achieve, the value you offer will often increase, but the capture ratio they'll pay you will be discounted. If you bring the timeframe too far forward, it may shrink the true value you offer but

---

[‡]In later seasons, there was a PC in the corner on the desk by the living room window, but at the time of filming, that shape and form had been remarkably consistent for two decades.

increase the likelihood of converting them. We find there's a Goldilocks zone for every offering, and it's critical to discover yours.

We also find it important to be transparent with your intended next sell as part of the customer journey: If people find what you offer valuable, they will buy from you again. When you openly present, "This is the type of relationship we would like to have with you," if it resonates, you'll see people drawn to it. If it doesn't, take that as loud feedback for honing your offering. When the context and intent are clear, leaving the power in the customer's hands as to whether they value it every step of the way, your sales team's effort in progressing the customer through each step can be greatly reduced.

As you map your customer journey, pay extra attention to the following three phases:

1. **Attraction**—It must map to their existing salience landscape but be novel in an important way to stand out as worth exploring.
2. **Initial purchase**—Find your Goldilocks zone for a high-margin but easy-to-say-yes-to test case that allows your customers the comfort and confidence they require to unlock their top spend.
3. **Know your exit**—We see so much long-term value get carelessly discarded by not being deliberate about when your customers stop being customers. Part of knowing your true value is not wasting your resources and reputation on doing business with people when they aren't going to receive that level of value from you.

How to Maximize What They'll Pay

If you want to build a ship, don't drum up the people to gather wood, divide the work, and give orders. Instead, teach them to yearn for the vast and endless sea.

—Antoine de Saint-Exupéry

People's values affect how much they will pay for your offering. But there's a big difference between the values *embodied* in one's actions and the *disembodied* values they espouse and talk about. We've all seen people say that they care about one thing and then behave exactly the opposite. This underlies Pricing Riptide #3: *What people say they value is different from what is embodied in their buying decisions.* It is critical to discern and eliminate these red herrings.[§]

Espoused Versus Embodied Values

To espouse any value, you first have to abstract it out of everyday life and represent it into a discrete statement. "I'm a *caring* person" and "I love *quality* things" are examples of values that can be distilled out of many different situations where you'll pursue one option above another. By disembodying them, we can remove them from everyday life, recognize their shared underlying patterns, and hold them up for examination and communication far easier than we could address all the various circumstances from which they were derived. Disembodying them also gives us important insight into additional aspects that we care about, which can be shared, discussed with others, and then taken back and applied to our next unique situation in the future.

However, when these values are placed in situ to life as lived, they become embodied. By physiological requirement, an embodied value must be prioritized. None of us can act on everything we value all at once, so we must arrange our embodied values in a laddered fashion, creating a value set. This arrangement is conducted in the current

---

[§]Unfortunately for this intent, most existing academic research into values falls under the methodology of classifying and correlating self-reported espoused values.

moment and environment. What is in one's current value set at any time can be inferred by what attracts their attention and motivates their action. At the macro level, it may look akin to Maslow's classic hierarchy. For example, "I love quality things" will play out very differently if you haven't had food or shelter for 10 days. However, the way embodied values are arranged in everyday life are far more limited and predictable, which is important for our purposes.

For example, let's take valuing career versus valuing family. It might be easy to gain a majority consensus (although not complete agreement) around the importance of valuing family above one's career. However, as these values are embodied, we'll observe a far more nuanced arrangement. If you were to miss one of your son's regular-season games to close the deal on a decade-long goal of selling your company, most people wouldn't bat an eye at that. But, if you missed your daughter's wedding to attend a monthly work meeting, most people would question your values.

In each of these situations, you're putting the embodiment of one value above another in light of a particular circumstance. Note that we're not saying by doing this, you don't value the other thing, you value them both. But when a conflict exists between a monthly work meeting and your son's regular-season game, we expect to see people play this out differently based on the idiosyncratic laddering of their embodied values, even when they both agree on the same espoused statement that family is more important than career.

How much someone will pay for what you offer is always consistent with where they rank it in their embodied values. After all, a purchase is simply a decision to pursue a selected course of action to get to a higher-valued state. Espoused values make great testimonials and can definitely be leveraged to create a social norm that will help you sell more of your offering. But they are too unreliable as an indicator of what someone might pay.

For example, in several cases, our portfolio companies have had their customers tell them that what they got from them was the "best thing that ever happened to them" or "fundamentally changed their life." These customers then go on to share that they would like to give something similar to their team, family, social group, and so on, only to inquire, "What do you have available for $100 per person?" There's never a need to contrast $100 with the description of "life-changing" if you understand and keep these two types of values separate.

Values Affect Perception

You are always trying to progress from your current state to a state you value more. After all, when was the last time you deliberately tried to get to a worse place than where you are?[*] Given our first-person perspective of the world, we tend to assume we see what's there, then choose to place our attention on the elements that are important to us, on the things we value. That assumption has proven to be wrong. Instead, from a physiological point of view, we only perceive the objects that make up our environment filtered by the pattern recognition[**] of what we value.

As any parent can tell you, the little humans we call children all have unique and sometimes comically innate interests that have nothing to do with the parents' background or the environment in which they're being raised. While the degree of environmental influence vs. innateness is still being debated and parsed, it is no longer a question of one versus the other but has now narrowed down to a matter of measuring degrees. Because different people have different innate predispositions to explore certain things above others, those dispositions lead to a feedback loop: what you explore, you understand at a higher resolution of detail, which in turn shapes how much you will prefer and value it.[††]

One cannot make sense of the world without perceiving it through the existing laddering of their values. For example, have you ever tried to help someone solve a problem, only to have them ignore your solution as an option altogether? To recognize a solution as viable when we get exposed to it, we must have already valued something close enough to

---

[*]Now you know the answer to "Why did the chicken cross the road?" He valued being on the other side more.

[**]Our ability to distinguish and group objects.

[††]This innate distribution of interest also offers possible criteria to identify potential customers more cost-effectively.

that solution to form the relevance realization required to take action on it.

Value Sets Create Expertise

Different ways of laddering our embodied values could be an advantage or a hindrance, depending on our goal and environment.[‡‡] Moreover, every individual has experienced their values evolving. What we think of as maturity is often simply progress in harmoniously integrating our embodied values at additional levels, in situ to the environments we find ourselves in. After all, it's the situations where we stop making satisfactory progress—or have achieved catastrophic failure—that tend to trigger the exploration and reprioritization of our embodied values.

In different industries and disciplines, we see similarities in embodied values by the individuals who choose to work there, contributing to the overall culture of that profession. Experts of any field share remarkably similar (though far from identical) value sets. To paraphrase a CEO friend who has successfully started and exited several biotech startups, Bill Gerhart, and his advice on finding investors:

> Contrary to common expectation, there is never a need to pitch your business to dozens of investors. All you need to do is meet with one, then go back and materially address all the things they point out as concerns or weakness in your plan before presenting to another. Not just on your PowerPoint slides, but in your company. It may take a few months or even a year, but by the time you've done that a few times, you have a company and strategy others are willing to invest in. Investors all value the same things; they will tell you what you need to do, so this persistent idea that you need to meet with dozens of them to get funding is just a waste of everyone's time.

[‡‡]This creates a reliable way to quickly identify and avoid charlatans. The charlatans will tell you to value something no matter what; quite different from someone with true mastery, who will inquire where you desire to go, and validate where you're starting from before suggesting what you should value to aid in your journey.

Obviously, when it comes to expertise, we're not suggesting skill, ability and many other factors don't play a major role. We're just pointing out that you're unlikely to gain the proverbial 10,000 hours on something you don't value (or, more accurately, on something you don't see as the best available instrument to get you where you value being). And while experts disagree all the time, they tend to zoom quite far into a subsection of their knowledge base in order to find something to debate in the first place.

Don't Cross the F-Line

Many long-term cash cows have been sacrificed simply because a business has crossed the Fair Line. Your anterior insula, the area of your brain that processes empathy and disgust, becomes highly activated when you perceive someone gaining an unfair advantage or being the victim of unfairness. This activation can quickly trigger the amygdala, creating a fight, flight, or freeze response. From firsthand experience, building a company that returns around 50 percent net profit is more than doable in many industries, but it's unlikely any public company could ever achieve it without a major backlash.

For example, Coca-Cola's leadership temporally crossed the F-Line when it decided to pursue a novel pricing strategy in response to a distribution problem. On hot sunny days in South America, Coke's vending machines would quickly sell out of ice-cold drinks before they could be restocked, resulting in lost purchases. Thinking from a traditional demand curve, the CEO had the ambient temperature sensor programmed into the vending machines that would increase the price from $1.00 to $1.50 on the hottest days. This crossed his customer's F-Line and sparked countrywide boycotts. Ironically, as behavioral economist Uri Gneezy points out in his book *Mixed Signals* (2023), Coke leadership could have easily avoided the problem by doing the opposite; that is, setting the price point of all machines at $1.50 and offering them on sale for $1.00 on cold days. Comparing your pricing strategy to your customers' laddering of embodied values can help prevent these unintended crossings of the F-Line.

In our experience, there are some things, like single-sourced life-saving drugs, that we would never suggest extorting a monopoly position on, no matter the price advantage. We never advise optimizing a price position when the buyer has no other choice. In Western values,[§§] removing someone's freedom of choice crosses the F-Line very quickly. This is a lesson many business leaders and politicians of all political parties should keep in mind, regardless of how noble the value they're pursuing.

Finally, controlling the marketplace comes with some of the highest monetization rates available. For example, Apple's App Store enjoys 30 percent monetization, and Google's ad revenue on YouTube is 45 percent. The more you can accelerate the success of others, the more you can charge them for doing so. But caution is always warranted: pigs get fat, but hogs get slaughtered. As you grow in size and dominance, so do competition and regulation. There are countless analogies warning against overmonetizing these positions, but the simplest thing we can suggest is to benchmark the total life cycle strategy with an appropriate risk profile mapped on top of it. Confronting how your price positioning reliably plays out over time can provide guidance to your top-line governor required to maintain and maximize long-term value.

Executive Conclusion

Nobody ever chooses the worst option.

Your customer's buying behavior is always consistent with their idiosyncratic laddering of embodied values at the time they buy. To conclude, they are buying an "inferior" product, is to impose your value set onto them—or worse yet, a set of values derived from an "objective view," which has yet to be discovered anywhere in nature. While objectivity is incredibly valuable, it's never held by a buyer while they buy. To plan your pricing strategy as if something is objectively

---

[§§]One of the biggest differences between Western and Eastern cultures is often thought to be a which value is held higher, individual rights or the needs of the collective.

more valuable than another is to ignore how the only people capable of paying you money perceive the world.

Espoused values are too unreliable to try to use directly for improving your monetization. However, they are useful to leverage as part of your pricing strategy. They can be effectively put to work with future prospects, not only through testimonials in marketing but also in establishing social norms to help build a higher-resolution picture among your potential customer base for the value you offer.

To achieve better monetization of your offering, focus on embodied values, and discern where your product currently ranks in your current buyer's idiosyncratic value set. Then make refinements to progress it up your buyer's ranking. Once you optimize value externally, there are almost always a handful of places where you can optimize the way you operate to produce that value with less time and expense.

CHAPTER 4

Re-Value Reliably

Do I not destroy my enemies when I make them my friends?
—Abraham Lincoln

When people first started leaving their digital cameras behind and took photos with their phones, they did so at the cost of quality. Early smartphone cameras were considered great if they squeezed in a couple of megapixels, and flip phones were even worse. But what users gained was the ability to capture more of the moments they wanted to remember, and that was valued more. Customers chose the same tradeoff when they first left their CDs at home in favor of lower-quality MP3s—the variety and accessibility of music were well worth it.

Many manufacturers of pocket cameras and CD players were heartbroken; why were people so readily embracing products that were clearly inferior? May none of us be so certain about the value we produce that we become blind to what our customers value even more.

Optimize to Your Size, Age, and Knowledge

*The question which we must ask ourselves is not whether we like or
do not like what is going on, but what we are going to do about it.*

—Winston Churchill

Company Size

The larger your company grows, the more value tends to leak through
the seams. This won't come as a surprise, as you are likely familiar with
the Pareto principle, a.k.a. the 80/20 rule; the majority of outcomes are
produced by a minority of the causes. So, the potential for internal value
capture is often expected. But few people truly confront the compound-
ing effects of the diminishing returns curve[*] and the effects of Dunbar's
number[†] on the Pareto principle as their organization grows.

For example, if you manage a team of nine employees, it's not
uncommon to observe that three of them produce 50 percent of the
team's output—as much as the other six combined. We know who these
top three are, and we do everything we can to retain them and grow
their contributions further.

But as British physicist and Information Scientist Derek John de
Solla Price observed, as the number of people engaged in creating the
output increased, the percentage of people creating that 50 percent
decreased consistently with the square root of the total number of
people. This matches the three to six example above, with three being
the square root of nine. But scale that team up to 100 employees, and
Price's Law suggest that only 10 of them are creating 50 percent of your
productive output.

It starts to get insightfully depressing in the range of 2,500, where
only 50 people are producing 50 percent of your output. That's not
to say that the other 2,450 are not hard at work every day; however,

---

[*]In economics, diminishing returns are the decrease in marginal output of a
production process as a single factor of production is incrementally increased,
holding all other factors of production equal.

[†]"Dunbar's number" is the notion that there exists a cognitive limit on human
groups of about 150 individuals.

most of that work is–*doing business with themselves*–"supporting" and "managing" those productive people, not directly producing what's required for your offering.

In one extreme case to illustrate the point, when a young Carl Icahn took control of a struggling company that manufactured rail cars, he fired 12 floors of managers in the New York office after talking to the COO who oversaw their actual revenue-producing products in St. Louis. To his great surprise, he didn't experience one unintended consequence of something not getting done consequently; it was as if they had never produced anything for someone outside the four walls of their own office building.

Over the years, companies have built many creative structures to address this phenomenon. Gore-Tex constructed separate offices for each of its business units, each with only 150 parking spaces. When people started parking on the grass, they knew it was time to split that unit into two. Many mega-companies are structured as holding companies; it's one way to keep the subcompanies as small as possible while still aggregating the profit and loss (P&L) of them all. And, of course, new leaders are often drawn to restructuring their departments in hopes of increasing efficiency. Sometimes, this comes out of necessity; other times, they're simply discarding a Ten of spades in hopes of drawing a Jack of Diamonds.

We're not suggesting that you should avoid growth. With personal experience in ventures building $15 billion facilities in the middle of nowhere, we've experienced firsthand that some value can only be extracted by operating collectively at a large scale. Nor are we saying you shouldn't try your best to create a company of nothing but those top employees. (Although if you did this, you would still see the same logarithmic distribution in productivity, albeit at a different level of absolute output.) What we are pointing out is how much internal value leakage becomes available for recapture as your company grows larger.

On average, we see about 50 percent of the earnings increase in our partners' companies come from stronger pricing power, and the other 50 percent comes from stopping internal value leakage—the unnecessary expense that doesn't contribute to creating or maintaining the value your customers pay for. But when we sort by company size, we see the mid- to large-cap (more than $2.0 billion) companies are weighted more toward stopping value leakage, particularly in a handful of key departments or business units. The small businesses ($1 to 100 million), meanwhile, gain more by improving their pricing power, with some help from refinements to the structure of their operations. Mid-size and small-cap companies fall somewhere between the two.

This distribution is almost expected; if a company grows to $2.0 billion a year in revenue, it has found a big enough vein in the gold mine to warrant value extraction at that scale. But we're continually surprised at how quickly the average manager can tell us where the most value is being leaked if they are only asked. It is true that their initial solutions as to what to do about it are rarely implementable, as they tend to be overoptimized to that person's department and push too many externalities onto others. But when Re-Valuing is managed well, we've reliably regained billions in lost value.

Company Age

If every cell in our body gets fully replaced over the span of 7 to 10 years, then why do we still age and grow old?

As it turns out, telomeres, the nonencoding ends of our DNA, shorten every time a cell replicates itself. Like the plastic bits on the ends of our shoelaces, telomeres prevent our DNA from unraveling. But they eventually wear down with replication, causing the cell to die. When skin cells start to die, you develop fine lines and wrinkles. When hair pigment cells die, you see gray hair. And as immune system cells die, you increase your risk of getting sick. When enough of these cells die, so does the whole body (Blackburn 2017).

Biologist Elizabeth Blackburn shares a Nobel Prize for her work in discovering a way for cells to replicate without the shortening of the telomeres. But, as you probably guessed, there's a catch. Those treated cells increase the chance of uncontrolled division, an effect commonly known as cancer. So, ironically, what causes our death in old age is the same thing that helps prevent the overwhelming likelihood of death from cancer before then. If a cell starts to divide uncontrollably, it uses up the remaining telomere length and dies. A sort of biological kill switch, so to speak. On the occasions that this doesn't happen, it often becomes the cancer diagnosis we're all familiar with.

Companies face a similar self-replicating dilemma.

What causes the decline and death of so many companies is either the unchanged replication of values or the uncontrolled mutation away from the core values that have proved to be successful. In the first scenario, the company's values go unchanged, but what their customers value and the environment the business operates in will continue to evolve. This creates a disconnect between the environment, customers, and what gets focused on by employees to produce their offering. But in the second scenario, many young companies never grow beyond a certain point because they haven't cultivated a set of self-sustaining values; value sets that replicate beyond the founders. Anyone can espouse a set of values, but it takes time and skill to Change to engineer and cultivate self-replicating values among a team that lives on over time.

For a company to live past a certain point, it must fix its values sufficiently in order to replicate them. But once fixed, part of what makes values self-replicating is that they attract employees with their own existing, idiosyncratic values that nest well into them. This, in turn, affects what they notice and attend to in plotting a strategy forward for the company.

At some point, the cells begin dying off and the traits of old age can be seen. For example, mature companies' values often lead to overanalyzing every decision to the point where no decision gets made, or the gap between espoused ways of working and how things really get done may widen. Both of these scenarios lead to politics reigning over competence.

These symptoms of aging can be seen most clearly when someone new joins. One might even be able to measure it by the frequency and duration of other well-meaning teammates in pulling a new hire aside to provide unofficial guidance on "how things *really* work around here." If this values gap gets wide enough, the friction of all the activity in the system can become greater than the productive output of the system itself. The increase of unspoken rules can end up running the show until the company has been sufficiently devalued against its stated purpose. At that time someone else will predictably acquire control of the whole thing to extract some set of component parts that they view as more valuable than what others will pay for the stated value the company is supposed to produce.

At a certain point, attempts for leadership to intervene will be at odds with their team's first-person sense of reality (*it won't match their salience landscape*). Like a compass that reliably spins but hasn't been adjusted for declination,[‡] efforts to plot a new course often assume a very different true north. Directions given are implemented in surprisingly adjacent and unintended ways. Things just seem predictably unpredictable as any forward progress fails to gain full traction. A case for periodic Re-Valuing is to avoid this tipping point well in advance.

Knowledge Commodification

We're in the late stage of the commodification of knowledge; however, the application of knowledge is expanding with ever-fragmenting specialties. One only has to go back in time half a career to see whole sectors where one could make a living out of studying a well-known, specialized body of knowledge, then be paid to representing that knowledge to a local group of individuals when they were in material need of it. Examples were small-town lawyers, real estate agents, travel agents, and so on.

The first domino, of course, fell with digitization. As information storage and distribution transmogrified from atoms to bits, the cost of printing and distributing physical material became comparatively high, while digital information came to enjoy extremely low variable distribution costs. This made the knowledge workers' lives easier; they could get quick access to the information, and their specialized knowledge was still required to find, discern, and recognize what was relevant. Those who didn't have that knowledge slowly started gaining

---

[‡]Declination is the deviation of a compass needle from magnetic north to true north and is a property of knowing where you are, not of where you are going.

access, but it took so much time to sort and understand what was salient; there was still plenty of value in the speed and confidence the expert could provide.

As search algorithms and then machine learning improved, so did our ability to self-serve. Today, for example, not only can you directly book almost any vacation in the world, but you have your choice between dozens of videos that walk through every activity or place you're thinking about visiting while there. If you want to get a feel for the neighborhood of a house you like, you no longer need to speak to an agent who will carefully curate their euphemisms to answer your questions. You can simply "walk" through thousands of photographs of the street and see for yourself. If you want to kill some time and watch a video, you get your own custom list curated by an algorithm. And these algorithms are created by people who can't even tell you why they think you'll find that set of videos relevant, yet you often do.

When Adam Smith wrote *The Wealth of Nations* (1776), he could not imagine a world where less than half the population wouldn't be farmers; that number is now ~3 percent. As the life cycle on one industry comes to an end, an enterprising few will always take those skills and apply them to a newly emerging problem or opportunity set.

As consumer-friendly versions of AI entered the public general awareness with ChatGPT and Tesla's Full Self-Driving, there has been speculation for new jobs groups like AI "Prompt Engineer" and business opportunities like leasing your car out for autonomous ride-sharing, generating revenue while you're inside your office all day. But it is important to remember all mature industries were once growth markets. Even if your industry is still on the growth side, this commodification of knowledge will affect your offering.

In more and more industries and situations, the "right answers" or "required strategies" are explicitly known already. But they still aren't getting utilized or implemented (i.e., *values not being embodied in situ to the current circumstances*). The trend we're observing among consulting firms, for example, is less value in being able to monetize their intellectual property (IP) or know-how[S] but an increase in the monetization potential for reliable application of that knowledge to materially affect an outcome that others cannot.

Executive Conclusion

The tension and inefficiencies between groups are inevitable in every way of organizing humans. But this tension can help optimize the precision of the output for the better, or it can lead to friction and distractions that have you leak what could otherwise be profits. The distribution of productivity follows a logarithmic curve, where a small number of employees generate a significant portion of the output. Internal value capture becomes more significant as your company expands and proactively addressing it can lead to significant recapture or prevention of lost value.

Your company must adapt its values and evolve them to prevent decline. To grow, a company must develop self-replicating values that go beyond the founders and attract employees with aligned values. But over time, aging symptoms for companies where their existing values have counterproductively mutated include overanalysis, expanding gaps between espoused ways of working and actual practices, and the rise of politics over competence.

If you're lucky enough to have your business grow old, tend closely to the early signs that parts of your company are optimizing to their own metrics—what they value—rather than the value your customers pay for. There is often a transparent thread that runs through every successful business and when employees lose track of it, the company leaves money on the table.

[§]Beyond the opportunity cost the acquirer would incur to self-generate.

Find Your Transparent Thread

Every single question you ask will trigger an emotional response on the other side.

—Chris Voss

Under the lights of a Broadway stage, the theatre director has the liberty to invent the world their characters inhabit. An actor walks out onto a blank stage and declares, "This town is Grover's Corners," and their proclamation is accepted by every customer that makes up the audience. Later, if a scene is set in the interior of a living room and a character walks off downstage left and returns a few moments later eating a snack, the director just tacitly established the location of the kitchen. Of course, if this were a real house, it's likely there would be more than one pathway from the living room to the kitchen. But any competent director knows that from now on, if a character exits to go get a sandwich anywhere else but downstage left, it will alienate the audience—leaving them slightly confused and annoyed, even if they don't quite know why.

When you have an established customer base, you've already formed an implicit compact with them, as referenced in Riptide #7: *Your past pricing creates future expectations... but your future isn't written yet.* Any changes will either enhance or undermine how they value your offering. Young companies are often so excited to discover a potential source of new customers that they don't consider the precedent they're establishing. Mature companies frequently find themselves constrained by expectations of more and more fragmented contingencies, each with its own set of rules for judging what you offer. Once created, these rules often become transparent, and we stop noticing them and the effects they cause.

This applies to your employees as well. Just as your customers never intentionally buy the worst option, we have yet to meet an employee who sets out to make the wrong decision or to make things worse. Almost always, your employees do the things they think are best at the time. The question, of course, is which embodied value they're prioritizing over which others. In our experience, the most destructive decisions in a business were born out of inattention, not malice. Malice does exist, and it's something we're all capable of, but it is not as common as it is assigned.

The challenge is that no employee will value what you tell them to; they'll value what gets them closer to where they want to be. But to listen to what an employee says they want would be to be caught in a version of Pricing Riptide #3: *What people say they value is different than what's embodied in their ~~buying~~ [work] decisions.* You see this every time the next generation enters the workforce. They come with a slightly different disposition in how they ladder their values, and managers, predominantly made up of a value set from a previous generation, don't know how to reliably motivate them. After enough time spent struggling goes by, managers end up asking and just implementing what the new generation requests—then proceed to see no change to the situation.

To discover what truly motivates someone takes more than just asking; it takes exploration, just like with your customers. Your employees see what they have been asked to optimize as an instrument, a pathway or an obstacle to progress to where they value getting.

Objectives and KPIs are important steps on the path to what your company is trying to achieve, or most frequently, what a subset of people have concluded will get the company closer to what they want to achieve. But these subgoals almost always come with an assumed *how* people will operate to achieve them—often based on the standard ways of operating in the department that's accountable for them. This results in people optimizing to their contributing parts, their department, not to the whole. It takes optimizing to the whole to truly deliver the value your customer pays for. There's a through line of value generation that runs through every organization, and it gets overlooked easily.

The Red Thread

In Sweden and other Nordic countries, there's an expression called the "red thread." It refers to the core idea or *through-line* of something that has everything make sense. This idiom comes from an ancient Greek legend in which the hero, Theseus, had to navigate a labyrinth to kill the beast that lurked inside, the Minotaur. No one had ever found their way out of the maze before. So a woman gave the hero a ball of red thread to unwind and follow back to find his way out, which he did after slaying the beast at the center (Webster 2021).

Every business has a similar thread that runs between what motivates their customers to buy, back through all of the internal departments and external partners required to reliably produce that offering. However, even in the best-run companies, that thread takes incredible twists and turns through the maze of competing priorities and accountabilities. And, indeed, in some companies, that thread seems to have been forgotten or lost altogether. You can easily recognize those companies where employees just do their part, unowning or uncaring how it all comes together for the value of the customer.

We find most of the companies we work with have gotten an overwhelming majority of the aspects of their business right. But like the hero going into the maze, we often see the existing way a company creates value their customers pay for going through a few unnecessary twists and turns. Leaked value lives here. These deviations are important to tend to; often, the difference between underperformance and top tier can be rather small when viewed from the whole. Opening up the opportunity to unlock a significant profit gain by addressing a relatively finite set of deviations in a handful of areas.

This is where having someone map your thread can bring outsized rewards. That is, draw a line through your organization back from the value your customers pay for (empirically validated, not assumed or prescribed) with *what* is truly required to produce that value today and reliably over time. This will be distinct from *how* you're currently producing your offering. The goal isn't to use this thread as a blueprint to reorganize your company. We've seen too many leaders go through the time and expense to restructure, only to have the same old issues pop up months or years down the road.

Instead, the goal is to illuminate this thread and see how it intersects with how you currently operate so you can identify the most fertile ground for step improvements. The biggest challenge, and the reason we suggest working with someone outside your company, is that the thread is often transparent and is easily lost. It's very easy to get distracted by *how* you currently produce your offering.

For the best explication of this underlying challenge, we turn to legendary Microprocessor Engineer Jim Keller. Jim has architected several of the major step changes in processing history. From coauthoring the instruction set that almost every server runs on in the world to developing a system on a chip for Apple's mobile devices or enabling AMD to become competitive with Intel, few people navigate both complexity and practicality the way Jim does. When partnering with Elon Musk on a bottom-up design for Tesla's Autopilot hardware, he describes this transparent thread phenomena in an interview with Lex Fridman (2020) as:

> *People are HOW constrained; "I have this thing, and I know how it works. And then little tweaks to that will generate something." As opposed to "What do I actually WANT?" and then figure out how to build it. It's a very different mindset....*

We find there are just too many opportunities to make things better, calling for teams' attention, and there's rarely the internal bandwidth or finances to address or optimize them all. But by discerning the true *whats*, those eyes of the needle, your team has no other option than to achieve in order to create the value that generates your revenue. The entire production chain of some of the most complicated businesses in the world can be distilled down to less than a dozen critical *whats*. Of course, the shorter you can make the distance between achieving each, the more value you can often retain as net profit.

How Do I Find My Transparent Thread?

By asking better questions. As Albert Einstein reportedly remarked, "If I had an hour to save the world, I would spend 55 minutes thinking about the problem and 5 minutes thinking about the solution." Effective problem formulation is an exercise in relevance realization, while solution implementation is often an exercise in cultivating embodied values.

In the era of fragmenting expertise, we have now entered the exponential part of the curve. Specialization is growing faster now than

---

*Emphasis added.

at any time in history (Malone 2011), offering both immense opportunities and a very challenging territory all leaders must navigate.

Specialization of expertise allows one to zoom in on any field, approach it from a particular value set, get their arms around it, and understand it in higher resolution to garner valuable insights and solutions. With specialization, however, comes overcertainty and overconfidence in one's answers and solutions (McGilchrist 2009). After all, the specialist must draw the bounds of what they focus on to master it.

Moreover, they must value some aspects more than others based on the original objectives their field of inquiry developed out of. So any expert answer, while valuable, invariably comes with implications and consequences that happen outside the focus of their expertise. This leads to unintended but highly predictable externalities, side effects, or consequences to the answers they advocate. By asking certain types of questions, you can cut through the competing priorities of fragmented expertise and true up to your transparent thread.

Adding additional weight to this dilemma is the fact that we have not finished recalibrating our metrics for dissenting or fringe opinions in today's world. For example, when the Obama administration embraced digital outreach through their petition system in 2011, they used a traditional threshold for public partitions of 5,000 people in 30 days. After being forced to make an official, on-the-record response to building a "Death Star" for military defense and letting Texas secede from the union, they ultimately raised it to 100,000. Today if someone holds a one-in-a-million opinion, it's relatively easy to rally a critical mass among the other 7,952 people in the world who share it.

A leader does not get to escape the unintended consequences of any decision. The larger the company, the more one department's externalities affect another department's entire field of play. And when companies push risk and cost onto their government, or society at large, past a certain point, those who push back end up doing so with an axe and not the scalpel required for a more optimal outcome for all involved.

There are no silver bullets. When optimizing, one cannot avoid pushing a bit of risk out and pulling additional opportunities in. That is to be expected. All important decisions are trade-offs.** If they weren't, they would be embodied actions already taken, not something requiring leadership to address.

Executive Conclusion

You Must Periodically Re-Value.

The field of play every business operates in is inherently dynamic. Even though your offering matched the environment and buyers when it was formed, over time, the whitespace between those three elements (buyers, environment, and offering) almost always emerges. Unmonetized value lives here. This whitespace is caused by employees and customers being driven by their own value sets. Employees do not intentionally make wrong decisions, but they prioritize different values based on their personal goals. Misalignment can lead to value leakage if not addressed. Similarly, customers value what you offer in your business based on how it aligns with their needs and aspirations. Managers often struggle with aligning these disparate value sets.

If you first look internally to decide what to address, each department will drown you in competing answers—all correct, but none as reliable as starting externally with the value your customers pay for. When you culminate around producing the value that generates your revenue and illuminate the thread that runs through everyone's scope, you'll begin to provide a framework for more effectively shifting how people operate, that is, the values they embody in their day to day.

Finding your transparent thread is about aligning your business's value with the needs and motivations of your customers and employees. It involves asking insightful questions, avoiding the pitfalls of overspecialization, and carefully managing the trade-offs inherent in decision making. Without periodic Re-Valuing, it's easy to be caught flatfooted when your customers start to value something else more than what you've optimized your company to produce.

**To paraphrase Thomas Sowell.

The Simple Process of Re-Valuing

There are just two questions to ask to attain success in business:
First, "What business am I in?" Second, "How's business?"
—Peter Drucker

In the 1960s, businesses predominantly defined themselves simply by the products they offered. Over cocktails, when you asked someone what they did for a living, you never had to brace yourself for an opaque, self-aggrandizing description. From the president to the warehouse janitor, every employee could say, "We make electric drills." Unfortunately, this clarity came at a cost. By building their entire identity around the product they produced, many companies missed the shift when their customer no longer needed or wanted that particular product.

In response, mission statements grew and reigned supreme in the 1970s. These brief descriptions of the company, what they did, and their objectives offered a way to broaden leadership's focus beyond products, putting those offerings into the context of their customers and market. Mission statements could even include any trends that the market may expect to see over the next three to five years. This shift toward forward thinking yielded enormous value.

By the 1980s, this focus on the future grew to include the idea of vision, providing more clarity on where the company was trying to go. And by the early '90s, discussions extended laterally, making purpose and values common conversations at every leadership offsite.

But in the wider selection of the possible environments a human can find themselves in, no value has yet proved itself so supreme that it can be blindly applied all the time. From a physiological point of view, if there was such a value, our species would have already evolved to embody it—and there would be no need to ever have debates about what to do or how to handle changing situations at all.

Side Note: Some people cling to the hope that there's a universal value we can rely on in every circumstance—love, for example. But to make this work, they often go on to define that value in a way that also includes the tension required from an opposing embodied value;

for example, while love is supporting others and being there for them, *true love* is also letting people fail and go it alone so they can learn for themselves. In other words, they simply redefine one value to include two embodied values in tension. Interestingly, enterprises that stand the test of time seem to find a way to create tension between relevant values, not just advocate for a predefined set of them.

Today, most corporate values are a variation of a theme wherever you go. It's easy to poke fun at the remarkable similarities in purpose, vision, and values between businesses as diverse as a high-growth SaaS company, a liberal Ivy League college, and a holding company that owns a coal mine. Yet to innovate is to ladder your embodied values in a different way than to optimize. So how can these all of these companies espouse the same values?

The Simple Process of Re-Valuing

1. Identify where and for whom you create the most *monetized value*.
2. Map your transparent thread through internal operations to the small *handful of whats* that are required to reliably create that value over time.
3. *True up* your company operations and the embodied values of those in each area that has the largest deviations.

While this process is fundamental, in our experience, many well-run and highly regarded companies would still require radical transformation to achieve it. We often see the same thing take people's attention away from the fundamentals; in pursuit of the next new thing, leadership took their eye off the basic blocking and tackling required to generate their core revenue.

When leadership beats the drum to value something more in one area, the go-getters will often flock to do so at the expense of abandoning something the leaders would never expect or desire. With no one intervening to keep the key revenue drivers on track, it's just a question of how long before you recognize the negative impact to the bottom line. The longer it takes (if it's obfuscated by positive capital growth, we have seen it take years), the more corrupted the relevance realization and embodied values of those remaining in the revenue-driving areas become. Truing up group relevance realization back to the fundamentals can then become a major endeavor itself.

By following the simple Re-Valuing steps in your business, you can more quickly discern the handful of areas in which you'll need to intervene as a leader[††]—simultaneously shifting your culture by discovering new and more effective pathways to produce your offering. The goal is to maintain focus on the one shared outcome that unites everyone in contributing to it. When Re-Valuing:

Do: Ask people where they think the company is leaking value.
Don't: Expect their solution to be viable outside of their department.
Do: Share with them the whats' that generate your revenue. While this might be obvious to you, most people are used to being graded only on a derivative of it that was relevant to them at some point in the past.
Don't: Expect them to believe you the first time you tell them you're committed to doing something different … or the second, or the third (they won't believe it until they see you and your peers as leadership embody your own values differently).
Do: Be willing to change how you embody what you value, which will change what you do and don't do.
Don't: Expect anyone to change how they embody their value set unless you first changed how you embody yours and have vividly demonstrated it through your own behavior.

[††]Lately, it seems like leaders are attracted to shifting their cultures to improve business results. But this can lead to a chicken-and-egg dilemma. If they don't pivot on the business results fast enough, they won't have time to create the culture they're looking to enable. But if they don't change the culture, those business results won't be sustained.

Don't Waste Time on Agreement

In the Re-Valuing process, the tensions between each group's internal value set will naturally lead to rightful debate. After all, one team's opportunity will be another team's obstacle. Each set of experts is only experts because they ladder their values differently. But there must be an overarching value set that everyone can own and operate under, that supersedes their own "right answers."

The more light you can shine on that overarching value set and the need to keep your transparent thread bright and tight, addressing what is required to generate the value you monetize with your customers, the easier it will be to create one shared overarching goal. As Coach Mike Krzyzewski told the top NBA players who were usually in competition with each other but now made up the U.S. Olympic basketball team for the 2008 games, "I don't want you to leave your ego behind in your own city; I want you all to bring it with you, just put it all under the ego of one U.S. Team."

The goal is to keep people rallied around progress toward the same revenue-generating outcome, *not just their own management metrics for indicators of how well their department is running.* Whether it be marketing versus sales, sales versus product, or product versus production, each must optimize to their own way of doing business. We're not suggesting reinventing the wheel with your yearly goals and metrics planning. We simply suggest supplementing this with unadorned clarity on *what* is required to generate the value customers pay for. After all, creating and delivering that value is the only reason everyone has a job in the first place.

In this way, the leadership team can share a common set of obstacles and opportunities—that is, shared relevance realization—that supersedes their own departments' scorecards.

Caution: Don't Cut Too Close

While ongoing improvements are often measured in bits, we suggest only pursuing areas of double-digit gains when Re-Valuing. If you see an option to save 3 percent, look harder for the place you're wasting 30 percent. Trust us, it's there. There have just been too many postmortems where we've seen prior cost-cutting efforts equate to a game of financial limbo. Reductions stayed for a while, only to be added back later—case by case, valid reason by valid reason. Where this didn't happen is where we found a new path that had everyone Re-Value how they thought about what they could produce—that is, reconfigured their embodied values—and pursued the step change in *how* they were operating.

We've also seen companies spend jaw-dropping amounts of money to prevent a one-in-a-million situation from happening just because it happened once before ... 20 years ago ... to someone who's not even around ... or wait, was that story even at *our* company? Obviously, this point can be taken too far; there are some risks that are always worth preventing, like loss of life. But humans aren't good at differentiating possibility from probability; we tend to over-attend to the vivid consequences and under-attend to the reality of minute probabilities. For example, the odds of dying at the beach because of a shark attack versus a riptide.

It's also far easier to optimize minor risk prevention in one department and, at the same time, let the bigger risks that cut across departments go unattended (same with capitalizing on opportunities). Fears often prevent new thinking to explore and pursue those areas. Executives who are willing to go on record and commit to providing air cover or even creating a quantified budget to cover any mistakes, if it enables actual value capture, can help teams break out of the fear of failure that often breeds stagnation.

Don't Play by Others' Rules

There's no other business exactly like yours. In our experience, the biggest reason companies deviate from their transparent thread is because people are playing by the rules of a game they're not in. Perhaps they're following the rules of the game they want to be in, or the rules they're most familiar with.

In an idealized game, every player knows the rules, and the winner simply played better than everyone else. But this will ring false to most successful people. You probably didn't achieve success by mastering the stated rules but instead by recognizing the existence of a new rule set that others seemed to be ignoring. You found a set that, when put into play, generated returns and results superior to those around you and, when further refined and scaled, led to a windfall of success. But in hindsight, this new set of rules seems obvious to all those who follow. Asking good questions and examining the rules people seem to be operating under will often point you to even more valued ground.

Executive Conclusion

Every company exists because it creates something someone else is willing to pay for—something they value. To the degree deviations happen from producing this, known or unknown, intentional or ignorant, money is lost. We advocate the Re-Valuing process because it works reliably, it matches how many companies were formed in the first place, and in our experience, it's the fastest and least bandwidth-intensive way to foment a shift and create a step change in your earnings.

Re-Valuing is a three-step process:

1. Identify where and for whom your business creates the most monetized value.
2. Map your transparent thread—the business's key outputs required to directly generate revenue.
3. Address and reconcile (or "true up") your company operations in areas showing the largest deviations.

This process acknowledges the diversity of values within teams and promotes a shared goal oriented toward value for customers. It's not about unanimous agreement but progress toward a common objective for which everyone is employed in the first place.

CHAPTER 5

True Questions

The Parable of Cash the Cow—Part II

Our Boy hadn't been back on the paved mountain road that led to The Grandfather's place since the night of his parents' car crash. Today wouldn't be the exception. Instead, the dusty old mule path made for a lovely—albeit steep—hike, which was good to clear his head and strengthen his legs.

As he walked, he oscillated between enjoying the view and wondering if he was wasting his time. It took a few hours to get into a hiking rhythm, to find the pace where his breath, heart, and forward progress fell into sync. When he finally arrived, the sun had just set. His grandfather looked up from splitting wood for the evening fire, and a big grin slowly bloomed across his face as he saw Our Boy walking down the driveway. After a warm hug and a brief stroll around the property fencerow, admiring the view, they headed inside to build the fire. While they waited for the kettle to boil, Our Boy described his dilemma.

"Everything is so interconnected," he said. "If I get rid of the low-margin buttermilk, I have a byproduct disposal problem for our high-margin butter. If I reduce the outer reach of our distribution range, which ends up running at a loss every time fuel cost is high, it'll cost us even more because we'll lose our economies of scale for feed. What makes it more frustrating is every time I ask my team what we might consider simplifying, I get a very short list of things in their area. But then proposals come in from each team to invest more in exchange for promised reductions in the future. A lot of times they have so many embedded and assumed dependencies to be realized in other departments. I feel like we do just as much business with ourselves as we do with others. Every time I ask about doing something different or new, I get a request for new headcount just to look into it!"

The Grandfather nodded rhythmically, not responding to anything in particular, as Our Boy continued late into the night. Instead, it was almost as if The Grandfather recognized the melody of a long-forgotten song. When Our Boy finally went quiet, his grandfather waited a long moment before observing, "You're not letting yourself ask the true questions."

"True questions?" asked Our Boy. Sinking back into his chair and struggling to process such an obtuse statement this late at night, he thought out loud, "So, answers are true or false ... but how can a question be true?"

"You already know so many more answers than I could ever fathom. The ones you don't are available at your fingertips. But without True Questions to guide where you look, you're unable to discern which answers you need."

Seeing the gears turning through Our Boy's eyes, The Grandfather continued. "True ain't right. True is what proves reliable with time, steadfast. When I true up a wagon wheel, I hone it so it rolls reliably. How well I do it can't be judged when I'm done working on it; how well can only be judged by how long it rolls over the side of this mountain."

"It's too easy to be *right*; to stake out a garden, trim down the world to only the bits you want to be there, creating and winning a game of your own making. What's right can be known, and people treat it like something they can own. But like other things we own, they tend to possess those who have them."

"What is true can only be searched for and revealed," he added.

They sat in silence. Eventually, The Grandfather rose from his chair, nodded goodnight, and retired to his bedroom.

Our Boy slept well in the mountain air and spent the next day sweeping the roofs and doing the chores he could tell his grandfather had stopped trying to handle on his own—not that he would ever ask a visitor for help with them. In the evening, they revisited many of the stories from Our Boy's youth, particularly from when his parents were still alive. As Our Boy headed out the next morning, his grandfather added one parting word of caution on what had motivated the visit.

"When you discover the True Question you're looking for, a smart boy like you may be humbled to realize how many people have discovered it before you."

When Our Boy reached the end of the driveway, he paused, looking at the dusty old mule path he had come up on, then turned to walk down the old paved road instead. As he rounded the bend that would remain forever imprinted in his memory, the scars of twisted metal on the rocks now looked muted. He paused, noting how much smaller the rocks looked now than when he'd sat there alone, waiting for the ambulance to come.

He breathed in and continued down the road. It was a strange feeling he was bringing down with him, a feeling that stayed with him as he entered the empty office the next morning.

After looking over all the existing reports and proposals with fresh eyes, he still didn't know what question to ask, or what strategy to endorse, but he called for a meeting first thing the next morning. All the division heads were in attendance, along with his old professor and various other advisers. He walked in, paused, surveyed the room, breathed in, and knew what he must do to move forward.

To be continued...

The Most Valuable Type of Question to Ask

It ain't what you don't know that gets you into trouble.
It's what you know for sure that just ain't so.

—Mark Twain

The word *true* shares the same Old English etymology with the word *tree*: to be steadfast, reliable. This is still represented in its current usage as a verb; "true up" means "to bring into alignment or position required to function as intended." In this sense, an arrow that flies straight is *true*. True is not *right*; we can come to almost any answer we want by changing the frame of reference to be *right*, that is, justified or acceptable.

In business, asking True Questions helps us cut through the stagnation often created by competing priorities. After all, each department may have the right answer from their frame of reference, and while these frames of reference are essential for everyday functioning of the organization, they rarely offer the clarity and understanding leadership needs in order to navigate unprecedented territory or make a decision on something emergent.

When you ask a True Question, you take a risk of hearing yourself answer the truth. Sometimes, the answer to a True Question will completely surprise you; sometimes, you know it already. Either way, it will alter the way you see what you're dealing with, and when you put it into action, the embodied answer to a True Question will alter you.

Example True Questions

"If you weren't already in this business, would you enter it today? And if not, what are you going to do about it?"
Father of management thinking—Peter Drucker

"Instead of just thinking I'm right, 'How can I know I'm right?'"
Global macro investor; founder of the world's largest hedge fund firm—Ray Dalio

"Is this decision a one-way or two-way door?"
Founder of Amazon—Jeff Bezos

"What important truth do very few people agree with you on?"
Venture capitalist and cofounder of PayPal and Palantir—Peter Thiel

"What if I could only subtract to solve problems?"
Author of The 4 Hour Workweek, angel investor—Tim Ferris

"When you worry, ask yourself, 'What am I choosing to not see right now?"
Leading expert on the protection of public figures—Gavin De Becker

"Did I spend today chasing mice or hunting antelope?"
Speaker of the House and architect of the Contract with America—Newt Gingrich

"What can we do today that we couldn't do yesterday?"
American scholar and national security expert—Henry Kissinger

"We have to confront ourselves. Do we like what we see in the mirror?"
America's most notable contemporary poet—Maya Angelou

"If today were the last day of my life, would I want to do what I am about to do today?"
American business magnate—Steve Jobs

"What good will [words] do you if you do not act on them?"
Wandering ascetic and religious teacher—Buddha

"If you are not trustworthy with worldly wealth, who will trust you with true wealth?"
First-century preacher and religious leader—Jesus

"Ask yourself at every moment, 'Is this Essential?'"
Roman emperor and Stoic philosopher—Marcus Aurelius

"Do you want to be someone, or, do something?"
Unsung hero and military theorist—John Boyd

"How am I going to live today in order to create the tomorrow I'm committed to?"
Life and business strategist—Tony Robbins

"What is the one thing I can do, such that by doing it, everything else is either easier or unnecessary?"
Bestselling author and founder of Keller Williams—Gary Keller

"If we're sitting here a year from now celebrating what a great 12 months it has been for you … what did we achieve together?"
Chief executive officer at Shake Shack—Randy Garutti

"What question should I be asking myself?"
Re-Valuing expert and author of this book—Adam Wallace

Your True Question:_____?
*How you would like to be remembered?*_____

A Word of Caution

True Questions are easy to avoid asking. It's easy for a company to become perpetually placated, to appease and give in to the gravitational pull to remain contentedly oblivious. It's tempting to form committees that review the same information and request more research, yet avoid accepting the transparent thread of what must be addressed.

The larger, older, and more knowledgeable your company, the easier it is to develop habits equivalent to corporate thumb-sucking, pacifying on a business binky: People doing their best today, getting surprised by something tomorrow, and shrugging their shoulders as to what could have been done differently after the fact.

Asking a True Question is not for the timid or the faint of heart. True Questions won't work when word-smithed or curated. To sand off every burr or snag before asking will only serve to dull your senses to the response.

They should be sharp, cutting, and to the point. True Questions can be humbling, requiring even the strongest among us to admit that we fall short of what we strive for, confronting what that is and seeking it beyond our past accomplishments.

They are not about understanding the past. While that can be a valuable pursuit, True Questions are designed to propel you forward. The following are some examples in this vein:

When Creating Something New

- What would you like to exist even if you weren't connected to it or around for it anymore?
- What are we all certain about in this field—and what would it look like if we successfully did the opposite?
- What might we do if we weren't afraid of failure?
- Would it still add value if done poorly?

When Continually Improving

- How do we know when to retire a metric?
- Who am I avoiding talking with?
- What indicators are we choosing to ignore?
- What is the worst case? Are we prepared?

When Assessing a Plan

- Take the case we failed; what did we miss?
- What would this look like if it were easy?
- What significant weakness outside of our control can we pull inside it?
- What must we do to ensure profitability in our bottom case?

When Confronting Uncertainty

- Why does this actually matter?
- What piece of this is in our control?
- If the worst thing that could happen happens, what would it take to get back here?
- Where have I abdicated my responsibilities to lead?

When Leading

- What is the most important thing?
- What will it take from me to make this possible?
- If not me, who?
- If not now, when?

True Cases and Cautionary Tales

The most common source of mistakes in management decisions is the emphasis on finding the right answer rather than the right question.

—Peter Drucker

Mid-Cap Tales: Netflix, JCP & AirB&B

Re-Valuing requires insight into what value your customers embody the most. In the following pages, we explore three example cases. Two are well-known companies that failed to assess how their new offering would be valued by their customer base. The third is the story of a senior leadership team who talked their way into the bedrooms of their customers, uncovering the value that motivated them to say yes to their unorthodox (at the time) offering.

Unbundling Gone Wrong

In the spring of 2011, 14-year-old Netflix was on track to break $3.0 billion in revenue, but leadership could already see the writing on the wall for their originating business model: shipping physical DVDs through the mail. And with streaming reliably growing year on year, their future prime product was obvious. To their leadership's great credit, they decided to take a proactive approach. Unfortunately, they neither considered nor tested how their customers would value their new offerings.

The internal strategy was quite solid: spin off the aging DVD product into its own entity that could be optimized to run smoothly until the inevitable decline. It looked to be at least a decade before reliable Internet would reach the most remote U.S. customers that the postal service reliably reached, so this offering was still far from irrelevant. Meanwhile, the name "Netflix" and the core team would stay with the growth offering, streaming. But the company's mistake was taking this sound internal strategy and pushing it into their customers' lives without considering how it would be received in their salience landscape.

At that time, Netflix's most popular offering was a $10 monthly subscription that offered both DVDs and unlimited streaming. So when customers received an e-mail that in a few months' time, there would be two separate services at $7.99 a month each (a 60 percent increase for those who wished to keep both), the F-Line had been crossed. Eight hundred thousand subscribers canceled, in many cases, more out of protest than because they couldn't afford the price increase. To make matters worse, the DVD service would be a new company with its own name, website, logins, and accounts. Customers were enraged, and Netflix quickly retreated back to the original combo.

Reports from inside the executive discussion boiled down to leadership's argument that "Netflix was a great bargain. We know ... some customers would complain but that the number would be small and the anger would quickly fade" (Sandoval 2012). One True Question that could have changed their fate: "Instead of just thinking we're right, how can we know we're right?"

Not Valuing What Your Customers Value

JCPenney was an old favorite of discount shoppers. So much so that one might have wondered if the value their customers paid for wasn't clothing as much as the joy of scoring a good deal. In 2010, smart investers with a proven trackrecord thought they could bring retail innovation back among the 154,000 employees at the 100+ year-old company.

Feeling the initial aging pressures of physical retail—which still remained dominant but was far from being the next novel thing— leadership understandably wanted to find a way to buck the squeeze of becoming irrelevant. Seeing coupons and discount sales as an embodiment of this progression, they decided to eliminate them altogether.

Instead, they introduced "Fair and Square Pricing" along with a new themed square logo and rebrand to JCP. In place of a dizzying array of discounts, markdowns, and limited-time coupons, there would be one fair list price. When it was time to run a back-to-school sale or the like, they wouldn't pressure people to run in to buy in a 24-hour window but offer those savings for the whole month. This, they thought, would create a reliable, predictable, and even more enjoyable shopping experience.

But this strategy neglected JCPenney's most valued offering from a salience landscape perspective: the dopamine hit customers would get when they dropped by the store and discovered a sale in a particular department. Total sales slumped aggressively; meanwhile, the company began to invest in new boutique brands like Sephora, hoping new customers would reconsider if JCP "was for people like them." But this didn't persuade enough new blood to replace their core customer base of aggressive bargain hunters.

Discovering Atomic Behaviors

Remember the first time you heard of Airbnb? The cognitive two-step you likely had to do when thinking about the unusual practice of renting out a spare bedroom in your house by the night? Now imagine being one of the first 100 people to ever choose to host strangers in your home on the platform. What must have you been thinking? That's exactly what the founders wanted to know themselves.

Technically the founders were the first hosts, making a quick site to advertise staying on a few air mattresses packed into their San Francisco apartment as a way to make extra cash during weeks of sold-out hotels. But they proved others would be willing to do the same when they managed to sign up new hosts in New York City. A culture of "couchsurfing" provided a pool of early adaptors to be able to monetize something they would be doing anyway. But what motivated these hosts, which embodied value did they strike a chord with, and how could they optimize their budding company to offer it better? Most importantly, how could they find out directly?

Noticing that what set the most frequently booked places apart was the quality of photos the host uploaded, the founders decided to offer these new hosts in NYC professionally taken photos for their listing. Of course, in this case, the founders would pose as and be the photographers. That way they could casually chat with the host about why they'd signed up and find out how hosting was going for them as they took pictures of the bedrooms and homes.

"We learned early on that being able to make a personal connection with the hosts was transformational for Airbnb" (Airbnb 2011). Instead of treating their service as a transaction, the way one might when buying or selling something in a classified ad, they realized they needed a way to create introductions that facilitated a personal connection. Out of this insight, a system of host and guest profiles became standard, allowing both sides to be comfortable with who the other person is and to be accountable for how they took care of previous bookings.

While obvious in hindsight, this innovation was key in allowing customer adoption to grow beyond a few quirky city users who were already letting strangers crash on their couches for a night. By the way, a decade later, they still offer to take photos for new hosts, though actual professional photographers are used now.

Large-Cap Tentions: Amazon

In the early 1990s, the brilliant minds at an MIT lab were disappointed. They were trying to add predictive functionality to a robotic arm. The objective was to autonomously catch a small ball tossed in the arm's general direction; thanks to Moore's Law,[*] they had expected there would be enough computing power to identify, track and predict the flight path of the ball. Identifying and tracking was working, but the prediction was not. The program was failing to calculate the flight path in real-time reliably enough for the arm to intercept the ball.

Looking for a different way to solve the problem, members of the lab reached out to their colleagues in a relatively new field that was taking off at all the major universities: cognitive neuroscience. How does the human brain handle this challenge? Computers were just starting to beat the occasional championship chess player, but they were still too slow to achieve a real-time task that the average four-year-old could perform.

---

[*]1965, Intel cofounder Gordon Moore predicted that the number of transistors on a microchip would double (thereby increasing the speed of our computers) every two years. His "law" holds true to this day.

But the researchers were surprised to learn that our brains don't predict the trajectory either. As a matter of fact, at the speed many balls travel in sports, our visual input devices—aka eyes—provide too few data points per second to perform an accurate calculation anyway. Instead, the brain only makes one binary prediction. Is the ball catchable? If yes, it triggers a routine, and we catch the ball. If no, we don't even try (Hawkins and Blakeslee 2004). This small insight led to a big breakthrough.

They stopped trying to predict the exact flight path of the ball. Instead, they predicted with great confidence the areas where the ball was *not* going. They then used this information to reposition the arm in real-time away from those areas, ultimately arriving in the same location as the ball in time to catch it.

Back in 2003, it was still considered highly suspect for a company to run off the capital it raised and not show any positive earnings year on year. But Amazon used this head start to position themselves in the right place to catch their intended ball when it arrived.

Most readers will be familiar with many of Amazon's unusual practices, like starting each meeting silently reading a Word doc summarizing the issue needing to be addressed. Or their "it's always day one" ethos. In disclosure, the main author has been an Amazon shareholder for years, as there are so many of the principles laid out in the book that they have embodied from their formation, despite being a low-margin large-scale business.

Three of these are worth highlighting as illustrations, along with one possible headwind. The latter we've been monitoring closely and are interested to see how it plays out in the long run. Regardless, Amazon has stayed true to its founding mission to offer the biggest selection, lowest prices, and most convenience.

Invest in What's True

To solve a problem, you have to frame it. Framing requires ignoring patterns in the environment that aren't salient to your goal. Things that go unchanged are the easiest to ignore. However, they can be the most valuable when building for the long term. In 2012, on the second day of Amazon Web Services' re:Invent conference, Jeff Bezos responded to a question about the changing future of technology at a fireside chat by articulating:

> I very frequently get the question: "What's going to change in the next 10 years?" And that is a very interesting question; it's a very common one. I almost never get the question: "What's not going to change in the next 10 years?"
>
> And I submit to you that that second question is actually the more important of the two—because you can build a business strategy around the things that are stable in time.... In our retail business, we know that customers want low prices, and I know that's going to be true 10 years from now. They want fast delivery; they want a vast selection.
>
> It's impossible to imagine a future 10 years from now where a customer comes up and says, "Jeff, I love Amazon; I just wish the prices were a little higher," [or] "I love Amazon; I just wish you'd deliver a little more slowly." Impossible.

When you have something that you know is true, even over the long term, you can afford to put a lot of energy into it.

That energy paid off, and a few years later, in 2015, after breaking 100 billion in U.S. revenue, Amazon leadership highlighted the following in their shareholder letter given the predicable downside that comes along with their new size:

> Some decisions are consequential and irreversible or nearly irreversible—one-way doors—and these decisions must be made methodically, carefully, slowly, with great deliberation and consultation. If you walk through and don't like what you see on the other side, you can't get back to where you were before. We can call these Type one decisions. But most decisions aren't like that—they're changeable, reversible—they're two-way doors. If you've made a sub-optimal Type two decision, you don't have to live with the consequences for that long. You can reopen the door and go back through. Type two decisions can and should be made quickly by high-judgment individuals or small groups.

As organizations get larger, there seems to be a tendency to use the heavyweight Type one decision-making process on most decisions, including many Type two decisions. The result of this is slowness, unthoughtful risk aversion, failure to experiment sufficiently, and consequently diminished invention. We'll have to figure out how to fight that tendency.

Navigating between polar forces is something built into the embodied values at Amazon. At one of Andy Jassy's first internal town halls, after he became CEO of Amazon (2022), he highlighted the case for ensuring embodied values are placed in appropriate tensions by sharing their "Leadership Principles":

Our leadership principles always have tension in them. And I think that is actually kind of a good thing and makes sense. But, if you think about a leadership principle like Have Backbone, disagree and commit: We don't just tell people that it's ok to disagree, if they think what we're doing [is] something wrong for customers, it's an expectation that you disagree.

And we encourage all of that debate and truth-telling. And yet at the same time, once we make a decision, no matter what side of the issue you were on, we all have to pull in the same way. It's hard enough in what we do to get things right for customers, but it's doubly hard if we're not all pulling in the same way.

…there is tension in the Leadership Principle, and that's because the world isn't simple and the problem we're trying to solve isn't simple.

Becoming the largest anything in the world opens the door to a level of scrutiny: some rightful, providing the impetus to do better, and some ignorant, casual disparaging remarks from those unaware of the very rules a business must follow in that industry or country.

Anyone who lives with the double-edged sword of fame can tell you that the more you get recognized, the harder it is to be seen. People instead recognize the pattern you embody and imbue you with the traits that come along with that pattern, regardless of the true you. Good or bad, unfair or fair, few will notice or feel sorry for those to whom this happens.

The same happens for companies too, but when was the last time you complained of buying too much stuff from Unilever?

We started wondering about this with Amazon in 2015 when we first started hearing our friends "confess" how much they order on a weekly basis. This was noteworthy since we'd never before observed people feeling guilty about how or where they bought their trash bags and paper towels. Since then, the level of scrutiny has increased, not just among some of their customers but up to the level of the U.S. Congress looking into some of their competitive practices.

If you have name recognition, it's often a no-brainer to leverage it for your next offering. However, at some point, the value created may be less than the increase in headwinds that come from the recognition of your size and earnings. This is something that Unilever gets to avoid with their branded products.

Small-Cap Creativity: Chameleon Collective

Imagine prevailing in the last battle to secure the independence of your country, only to watch as the unity built out of the blood of your brothers and sisters slowly begins to fragment. After the Revolutionary War, the United States was not so united. When each state sent two representatives to Philadelphia 15 years after winning their independence, mutual distrust was the main thing that constituted the document that would later be codified as the U.S. Constitution.

People knew the unintended flaws of every way of organizing. If you give the general populous direct participation, the government will swing wildly along with the emotions and fads of the moment, creating scapegoats and quixotically charging at windmills. If you put seasoned statesmen in charge, they will always be too disconnected from the people and, thus, from the effects of their decisions, inevitably corrupting the system to their own advantage. If you rely on a committee to make decisions, it will never agree on anything fast enough to respond to emergency situations. And although a monarchy offered the ability for things to move quickly, too much blood was spilled, fighting the tyranny that comes from one person having a sovereign rule to ever consider it again.

Regardless of the founders' aspirations, they knew what would be true over time. Checks and balances were born not out of some grand design, but out of confronting the true nature and unintended consequences of every possible system of governance.

It was another former Brit, Freddie Laker, who now called America home over 200 years later. He created his fourth business with a similar set of checks and balances. Having borne the imprints of success and a couple of scars of failure along the way, he was enjoying a respite from founding companies by filling a chief marketing officer role for a while. Vowing to never, ever, ever start a company again, he began envisioning himself as a marketing mercenary for hire, accepting a series of interim executive roles where he specialized in building small, lean internal marketing departments from scratch. So when a friend approached him to start a company so they could work together and offer more resources at a scale beyond just the two of them, Freddie had been on a self-reflective journey to know the unconventional constraints that must be put into place to entertain this possibility.

Having sold one of his previous businesses to the marketing firm Sapient, Freddie had spent the next several years as a VP in a large firm. He knew the risk (and, frequently, the waste) that came with a giant payroll hanging over the owner's head—not to mention the expenses of a physical office and all the miscellaneous costs that add to the pressures and stress of running a traditional agency.

Regardless of success and aspirations, Freddie knew that at the end of the day, services would get sold to keep the client happy, even when they weren't valuable. And people would spend a certain amount of their time on bullshit projects that they knew would make zero difference in their client's actual business. He wanted to continue making the New York money he'd grown used to. But not to live in New York, where that amount of money doesn't mean as much as it does elsewhere.

Most importantly, Freddie didn't want to work for someone else again, only with people he personally respected and who respected him. So Freddie and his partners began to codify the "Rules of Engagement" for what would become a capitalist collective—a company in service to the people in it (versus a bunch of people in service of the company):

1. The company is not designed to make money, it's designed to make money for those who are in it.
2. No matter who the CEO is, or who makes up the company leadership team at the time, the client delivery structure will be reorganized each time, with the person who owns the client relationship at the top.
3. A remarkably low 5 percent of people's revenue and 5 percent of their time goes to the collective for consolidated services like billing, legal, IT, case studies, and asset creation.
4. With business development, 5 percent of the revenue goes to the person making the introduction, and 5 percent goes to whoever leads the closing of the sale.

What Freddie didn't predict, though, was just how many other executive-level resources jumped at the chance to join the collective. He had fulfilled his personal desire to be his own boss while avoiding the time suck of the operational "stuff," smoothing out the business development boom-and-bust cycle, and eliminating scalability issues so he could perform whatever scope his client required. But by solving these things for himself, he attracted the type of people many firms want but can never hire—leading to his little experiment growing 30 percent year on year.

Within a few years, his collective saw the early warning signs of inefficiencies from letting too many great people join, so they implemented a limit of 150 members. Then, they began exploring how to replicate other symbiotic collectives in adjacent skills and industries. No matter how this experiment pans out, Chameleon Collective will leave a memorable legacy for those in it—and if their Glassdoor ratings count for anything, a different model of work worth exploring for high-talent professionals.

Epilogue: The Parable of Cash the Cow–Part III

What is the meaning of it all?

—Richard Feynman

How the Parable Ends

The Grandson goes to the farm every day on his way home from school to do his chores. His father runs the place and incentivizes the Grandson to work smarter by giving him one big job each day. The more efficiently he can accomplish it, the faster he can go onto anything else he wants to do. Often the Grandson tries to do it as fast as he can so he can join his grandfather on his daily walk along the fencerows.

After scooping out the calf barn in record time, the Grandson sprints to the courtyard just in time to catch Our Boy heading toward the back forty. Now a grandfather himself, Our Boy still comes every day to check on the herd during feeding and give tours to anyone who wants to learn from their operations. Today, his Grandson is particularly excited to ask about something he'd heard from an exchange student at school. His new friend had seen a picture of the statue of Cash and remarked that this cow was on every milk carton in his home country.

"Indeed, it is," Our Boy says proudly, describing the name and likeness of Cash have been licensed overseas. "When I was a few years older than you, I took over running this whole place. I wanted to save the farm, and I thought growth in size was the only way to do that. Then I found myself in a similar situation to the one my grandfather had been in. We were making more money, so the problems weren't exactly the same, but they certainly rhymed—just with more zeros and scrutiny on missteps."

Our Boy went on to share the story of his trip up the mountain and what his grandfather had told him. "When I left your great-great-grandfather's house, I asked myself what I wanted my life to be about, but no answer came. When I got to the end of the driveway, I asked what I was avoiding, and the answer came instantly. So, I had to walk down the road I least wanted to travel. Later, when I thought about the week ahead and asked what I didn't want to address, I knew exactly what that was. By the time I got back to my office, things stopped being about deciding what I wanted; they were about accepting what I was compelled to handle which what was right in front of me.

As soon as I got my team together, I knew our problem wasn't our lack of solutions; we were drowning in them. Our real problem was a lack of clarity for the things that bound us together. I saw that most people's time and attention was spent on what they saw as the problems in the way of where they themselves wanted to go. For years I thought my job was to decide the most valuable path and convince others to value walking it. That worked in the early days but stopped being effective at a certain size.

When we looked at the unique value we had to offer—like being the premier hometown dairy—we all saw that when we expanded our range, we became just one of three different milk jugs on the shelf. No one had a personal connection with us.

But when we looked even further outside of our distribution range, what we found people valued about us completely shocked me. I would never have thought of the idea to license Cash's name and likeness. I valued Cash, and I valued how special her milk was. But in a million years I would have never thought to value what others did when they saw her; the quintessential dairy cow. This still boggles my mind as I had never seen an all-black dairy cow before or since. It really taught me to never be so certain I knew, or understood what other people valued, that it would blind me to a better deal.

So I started asking my team *True Questions* as they came up. This slows down our automatic impulse to respond to every never-ending flow of problems generated by all of our competing goals and metrics. Instead, we started investing our focus on identifying *what* would we have to achieve to truly excel at the game we were in. Then I had everyone bluntly put on the table what it would take from them to make that predictable, and *how we might stack the deck for it to go right.*

About a third of the things that got mentioned had often been addressed already; the person bringing it up just wasn't aware (although they would have spent their bandwidth being concerned with it). The next third were small, often mismatched expectations or minor obstacles that only took a bit to address and sort out. The final third, though, were actual issues worth addressing. While there were a couple dozen at first, as we discussed them, they boiled down to just a few underlying issues we recognized had long been around and debated for a while. But none of us, myself included, were actively resolving them.

After becoming a bit disgusted by how many of these issues were actually within our control, we implemented our own version of the "two-minute rule." Whenever someone started to assign responsibility to a group that wasn't in the room, they had 120 seconds to confirm the issue—then they had to invite a key person from that group to help address how to achieve the *what* we were going after. We discovered that we could often address issues for each other's area easier than we could address some of them for ourselves. And in a few cases, this led to bringing some of our suppliers and vendors in on the discussions.

That led me to start asking our suppliers and vendors what they were hoping to achieve with our relationship and what was the biggest thing in the way of achieving it. To my surprise, several of their challenges we could solve with marginal effort, and, in turn, they were often better positioned to address some of our underlying issues we were struggling with. It was surprising how fast we could solve things when we were willing to think outside of our own four walls.

This ended up leading me to one of my biggest unanswered questions—why didn't the former CEO who introduced me to the blending strategy ever implement it himself at his own dairy? As it turns out, the economics and operational disruption to a large, established dairy farm were very unattractive until they had one complete herd ready to go. This could take 9 to 24 months of breeding, buying, building, and getting 120 cows ready. But once they were producing, that herd would be worth the same as 120 grand champions—that is, two or three times more than what people would pay for the individual cows.

So that's what our farm became. It let us keep our local market, as no matter what profile of herd we're currently breeding, we have the evergreen testing in-house to maintain a consistent profile for our local supply. Now we've shipped herds to every corner of the country, not only keeping an 18-to-36-month backlog filled, but being the producer of the most grand champions in the country. Which is part of what continues to make Cash's likeness so valuable in other countries that it's not practical to ship a herd, some 60 years later...."

After having to pause to find his footing while crossing a drainage ditch, Our Boy places his hand on the Grandson's shoulder for stability and remarked,

> I guess I'm the old-timer now ... I ask at least one True Question every day. But I still don't know if it's the actual question that matters, or just my willingness to be humble enough to ask. Heck, maybe it's just being willing to hear the answer I already know but haven't wanted to accept. Whatever it is, when I move forward with the answer that comes, it seems to lead me to my most valuable path.

With his hand still on his Grandson's shoulder, a smile blooms across Our Boy's face. "And today, that path is walking the fencerows of our family farm with my grandson."

How Will Your Legacy End?

Your next step is simple. You are the first domino.

—Gary Keller

You are the only expert that matters. Others cannot purport to know what you should do—nor do they have to live with the consequences of getting it wrong. This is an inherent dilemma that all leaders face. Whether you're accountable for thousands of people or just yourself, the challenge of scouting and mapping out the journey ahead is yours alone.

1. If you simply follow what things are worth to you, you will miss out on what others are willing to pay and contribute. But if you only follow what other people value, you're unlikely to find the meaning to sustain your pursuit.

2. When you're willing to confront your own Transparent Thread, the road untaken often becomes your most valuable path. The answers to True Questions will lead you into unexpected territory, where the biggest gains often come from the adjacent places where you least likely value looking for them.

3. As you discover your own value set—the one that enables you to successfully navigate your chosen path—by all means, share it. But resist the temptation to try and clone your values in others. Imposing yourself onto someone else's journey will only serve to mislead them from following their own.

And remember, nothing undermines your journey more than ignoring the truth. Through the prism of hindsight, once-accepted justifications often fade away, but what proves reliable over time will always be valued.

Godspeed Ronan,

Love, Dad

P.S. For everyone else, we are honored that you spent your time reading this monograph on Value. We truly hope it sparked one worthwhile idea that made it a fair exchange for your time. If you're willing to share what that was, or if there's anything we can ever provide to aid your journey, you can reach us at Contact@AdamWallace.com.

References

Airbnb. October 5, 2011. *Airbnb Free Photography: Celebrating 13,000 Verified Properties and Worldwide Launch.* https://blog.atairbnb.com/airbnb-photography-celebrating-13000-verified/ (accessed November 1, 2022).

Amazon. 2016. "2015 Letter to Shareholders." *sec.gov.* www.sec.gov/Archives/edgar/data/1018724/000119312516530910/d168744dex991.htm (accessed November 1, 2022).

Amazon News. April 1, 2022. *Andy Jassy Discusses Amazon's Leadership Principles and More | Amazon News.* https://youtu.be/0XznxAFPM10?t=1096 (accessed May 15, 2022).

Beck, J.S. 2020. *Cognitive Behavior Therapy: Basics and Beyond.* New York, NY: The Guilford Press.

Bezos, J. November 29, 2012. *2012 Re:Invent Day 2: Fireside Chat With Jeff Bezos and Werner Vogels.* Interview by Werner Vogels. www.youtube.com/watch?v=O4MtQGRIIuA.

Blackburn, E. 2017. "The Science of Cells That Never Get Old." TED.

Chan, K.W. and R.A. Mauborgne. 2005. *Blue Ocean Strategy.* Boston: Harvard Business Review Press.

Christensen, C.M. 1997. *The Innovator's Dilemma: When New Technologies Cause Great Firms to Fail.* Boston: Harvard Business Review Press.

Collective Equities. January 1, 2021. *Home Page.* Collectiveequities.com (accessed March 17, 2021).

Cytryn, K.N. 2001. *Reasoning and Decision-Making Related to Health and Illness* [PhD Thesis]. Canada: McGill University.

Damasio, A.R. 1994. *Descartes' Error: Emotion, Reason, and the Human Brain.* New York, NY: G.P. Putnam.

Florida Museum of Natural History. December 31, 2022. *International Shark Attack Files.* www.floridamuseum.ufl.edu/shark-attacks/maps/world-interactive/ (accessed December 31, 2022).

Gladwell, M. 2004. "Choice, Happiness and Spaghetti Sauce." TED. Monterey, California.

Gneezy, A., U. Gneezy, and D. Lauga. 2014. "A Reference-Dependent Model of the Price–Quality Heuristic." *Journal of Marketing Research,* pp. 153–164.

Gneezy, U. 2023. *Mixed Signals: How Incentives Really Work.* New Haven: Yale University Press.

Godin, S. September 19, 2016. *How to Differentiate.* Interview by Kirby Hasseman. www.youtube.com/watch?v=2T_k98bsaas.

Godin, S. 2003. *Purple Cow: Transform Your Business by Being Remarkable.* New York, NY: Portfolio.

Hawkins, J. and S. Blakeslee. 2004. *On Intelligence.* New York, NY: St. Martin's Griffin.

Kahneman, D. and A. Tversky. 1979. "Prospect Theory: An Analysis of Decision Under Risk." *Econometrica* 47, pp. 263–291.

Kahneman, D. 2011. *Thinking, Fast and Slow.* New York, NY: Farrar, Straus and Giroux.

Keller, J. February 5, 2020. *Moore's Law, Microprocessors, and First Principles.* Interview by Lex Fridman, 1:04:551:05:10. www.youtube.com/watch?v=Nb2tebYAaOA.

Lewis, M. 2004. *Moneyball.* NY, New York: WW Norton.

Malone, T.W., R. Laubacher, and T. Johns. July–August 2011. "The Age of Hyperspecialization." *Harvard Business Review.*

McGilchrist, I. 2009. *The Master and His Emissary: The Divided Brain and the Making of the Western World.* New Haven: Yale University Press.

McRaney, D. May 5, 2013. *Survivorship Bias.* https://youarenotsosmart.com/2013/05/23/survivorship-bias/ (accessed June 15, 2022).

NOAA. December 31, 2022. *Surf Zone Fatalities: 2010 Through December 31 2022.* https://noaa.maps.arcgis.com/apps/dashboards/60d29733f7e44d49a25cfe1178ea6798 (accessed December 31, 2022).

Peterson, J.B. 1999. *Maps of Meaning: The Architecture of Belief.* New York, NY: Taylor & Frances/Routledge.

Sandoval, G. July 11, 2012. *Netflix's Lost Year: The Inside Story of the Price-Hike Train Wreck.* www.cnet.com/tech/services-and-software/netflixs-lost-year-the-inside-story-of-the-price-hike-train-wreck/ (accessed November 1, 2022).

Simon, H. 2015. *Confessions of the Pricing Man: How Price Affects Everything.* New York, NY: Springer.

Smith, A. 1776. *An Inquiry Into the Nature and Causes of the Wealth of Nations.* London: W. Strahan and T. Cadell.

Thiel, P. and B. Masters. 2014. *Zero to One: Notes on Startups, or How to Build the Future.* New York, NY: Crown Business.

UBS. 2019. *Nobel Perspectives: Daniel Kahneman.* www.ubs.com/microsites/nobel-perspectives/en/laureates/daniel-kahneman.html (accessed January 29, 2023).

Voss, C. 2018. *Skilled Negotiation Strategies.* Interview by Dena Burton.

Webster, T. 2021. *Find Your Red Thread: Make Your Big Ideas Irresistible.* Vancouver: Page Two Press.

About the Authors

Adam Wallace, the American, has spent years unlocking pricing power for products and services. After more than a decade as a corporate fixer, joining Fortune 100 leadership teams to capture additional value on multibillion-dollar ventures, he now serves as an interim executive and board member for private companies. Adam grew up in a two-story log cabin outside of Nashville, built by his seventh-generation grandfather prior to Tennessee becoming a state.

Adam Wallace, the Australian, is a multiple *The New York Times, USA Today*, and Amazon bestselling author. He has sold over five million books, with a mission to entertain and inspire millions around the world. Adam has a unique gift for composing stories that are interactive, teach key skills, and, most important of all, entertain.

Index

Agreement, 70
Airbnb, 83, 84
Amazon, 84–88
Attraction, 45

Bezos, J., 85
Blackburn, E., 56
Buying, 23–24, 29, 32, 51

Cash and cow, 10–15, 73–75, 91–94
Chameleon collective, 88–90
Churchill, W., 54
Coke leadership, 50
Commodification of knowledge, 58–60
Company age, 56–58
Company size, 54–56
Customer alumni, 43–44
Customer value, 82–83

Declination, 58
Differentiation, 37–38
Drucker, P., 67, 81
Dunbar's number, 54
Dynamic stage, 16

Einstein, A., 32, 64
Embedded stage, 16–17
Emergent stage, 16, 19
Espoused vs. embodied values, 46–48
Expertise, 49–50
Expert predicament, 35–37

F-Line, 50–51
Ford, H., 16
Fridman, L., 64

Gatekeepers, 40–41
Gerhart, B., 49
Gladwell, M., 23–24
Gneezy, U., 50
Godin, S., 38

Holiday, R., 9

Initial purchase, 45
Insurance, 42

JCPenney, 82–83

Kahneman, D., 30
Keller, G., 95
Keller, J., 63–64
Kennedy, J. F., 5
Knowledge commodification, 58–60
Know your exit, 45

Leadership principles, 87
Levitt, T., 24
Lewis, C. S., 40
Limbic system, 29
Lincoln, A., 53
Loss avoidance, 41–42
Loss leaders, 40–41

Marks, H., 29
Monetization curve, 16–20, 17f, 18f, 20f, 52
Moneyball strategy, 34
Monsanto, 34
Moore's law, 84

Netflix, 81–82
Novelty, 34–35

Offering, 5–6

Prevention of obstacles, 42
Pricing, 26–27
Pricing riptides, 21–27
Prospect to customer, 41–42

Recognized satge, 17
Red thread, 62–64

Re-valuing, 3–4, 67–70
Rules of Engagement, 89–90

Saint-Exupery, A. d., 46
Salience landscape, 34–35, 37, 81
Seinfeld, J., 43
Smith, A., 59
Solla Price, D. J. d., 54

Transparent thread, 64–66
True Question, 76–80
Twain, M., 76

Values affecting perception, 48–49
Voss, C., 61

Wilde, O., 21

www.ingramcontent.com/pod-product-compliance
Lightning Source LLC
Chambersburg PA
CBHW061830220326
41599CB00027B/5247